the God
EMPOWERED

*How Strong Women Can Help Their Husbands
Become Godly Leaders*

K. B. Haught

All Scripture quotations, unless otherwise indicated, are taken from the Holy Bible New international Version®. NIV®. Copyright © 1973, 1978, 1984 by International Bible Society. Used by permission of Zondervan Publishing House. All rights reserved.

Scripture quotations marked "KJV" are taken from the New King James Version. Copyright © 1982 by Thomas Nelson, Inc. Used by permission. All rights reserved.

Scripture quotations marked "NLT" are taken from the Holy Bible, New Living Translation, copyright 1996. Used by permission of Tyndale House Publishers, Inc., Wheaton, Illinois 60189. All rights reserved.

Scripture quotations marked "Amplified" are taken from the New American Standard Bible®, Copyright © 1960, 1962, 1963, 1968, 1971, 1972, 1973, 1975, 1977, 1995 by The Lockman Foundation. Used by permission. www.Lockman.org.

Cover design by Jerry Cooley

Library of Congress Cataloging-in-Publication Data
Haught, Karen, 1957 –
The god empowered wife: how strong women can help their husbands become godly leaders/ Karen Haught.
        p. cm.

1. RELIGION / Christian Life/ Love & Marriage 2. RELIGION / Christian Life / Women's Issues 3. RELIGION / Christian Life / Family

Printed in the United States of America

Copyright ©2008 K. B. Haught
ISBN-13: 978-0-615-17624-6
ISBN-10:   0-615-17624-0

Library of Congress Control Number: 2007903233

kbhaught@godempowered.com
www.godempowered.com

To Jim,
my husband, my lover, my provider,
the man who prays for me continually,
my companion on the journey,
my best friend forever.

☙ ❧

The world and its desires pass away, but the woman who does the will of God lives forever (from 1 John 2:17).

How to Use this Book

This book was written to address the unique challenges that strong, dominant women experience in marriage. My sisters of a more submissive nature, particularly those married to dictatorial husbands, might find it hard to read because the stories and examples are from marriages where the wife is in charge. The biblical principles are the same, but the practical applications are different.

Women who are dealing with life-dominating sins in their husbands, such as drunkenness, drug abuse, pornography, or adultery will require additional information on prayer and discernment that is beyond the scope of these pages and has been reserved for another book. The concepts presented here, however, are the foundational truths upon which the wisdom to overcome even these difficult situations is built.

I couldn't possibly have included every type of marital scenario, so I urge you to use this book in a small group setting to discuss, share, and role play. Each chapter closes with homework/discussion questions to answer in your journal, a short prayer for you, and an even shorter prayer for your husband. Write his on a sticky note and put it where he can see it each week, but leave it up to God whether he actually prays it or not.

God's Word—the Bible—tells you all you need to know to help your marriage become glorious if you learn to apply it properly. God doesn't want you to become a cookie-cutter wife and He certainly doesn't want you to become a doormat. He *does* want you to reflect His love into your marriage through the mirror of your unique personality and gifts.

You begin doing that by first understanding your most important goal in life must be to please God. A friend once described that as "wanting to please God more than you want to breathe." It's not a one-time repair job. It's an ongoing, life-long journey.

As you start to see the fruit of the Spirit in your marriage, teach other women what you have learned. You don't have to be a seminarian or a certified counselor; you just have to know and believe God's Word is true—and be willing to act on it. I'm not the expert, God is; and if these principles work for you, it's because they're based on His truths.

I would love to hear about your "God Empowered Wife" journey. If you have a testimony to share, no matter how small, send it to me at kbhaught@godempowered.com. It might be just the encouragement other women need.

Blessings,
Karen Haught

GROUP STUDY SCHEDULE GUIDE

Suggested 12-week small group schedule
Week 1:   Introduction, Chapters 1-3
Week 2:   Chapters 4-6
Week 3:   Chapter 7
Week 4:   Chapter 8
Week 5:   Chapters 9, 10
Week 6:   Chapter 11
Week 7:   Chapter 12
Week 8:   Chapter 13
Week 9:   Chapter 14
Week 10:   Chapter 15
Week 11:   Chapters 16, 17
Week 12:   Discuss 16, 17, and close

Suggested 9-week small group schedule
Week 1:   Introduction, Chapters 1-4
Week 2:   Chapters 5-7
Week 3:   Chapter 8
Week 4:   Chapters 9, 10
Week 5:   Chapter 11
Week 6:   Chapters 12, 13
Week 7:   Chapters 14, 15
Week 8:   Chapters16, 17
Week 9:   Discuss 16, 17, and close

If you have a longer period together, spread the first chapters across several weeks. The more time you take to think about and apply these concepts in your marriage, the more likely they are to impact your life.

Suggested 6-week small group schedule

Week 1:   Introduction, Chapters 1-4
Week 2:   Chapters 5-9
Week 3:   Chapters 8-10
Week 4:   Chapters 11-13
Week 5:   Chapters 14-17
Week 6:   Discuss 14-17, and close

Author's Terminology Notes

Christian: *There are many perceptions of the word "Christian" in the world today. For some, it means simply trying to be a good person. For others, particularly non-believers in second and third world countries, it has taken on the halo connotation of "American" immorality. Even among Christian denominations, there is much disagreement about the qualifications for being a Christian. For clarity's sake, then, I have chosen to use the terms "believer" or "follower of Jesus" to describe a person who has made a personal choice to believe in and on Him as their Savior, regardless of denomination, ritual, nationality, or background.*

Strong: *Strength comes in many forms, and both dominant and submissive women can be strong in the sense of having a solid foundation, unwavering conviction, commitment, and confidence. However, when I use the term "strong woman" here, it refers to someone who tends toward being assertive, bold, outspoken, and even controlling. In short, someone who is passionate about her opinions and perceived rights. Sometimes an outwardly passive woman can be strong in this sense, through manipulation.*

Meek: *When I use the terms "meek" and "passive" here, it is not in the sense of a woman who reflects Christ-like humbleness, quietness, modesty, and gentleness. Rather, it is referring to someone who is timid, shy, and reluctant to assertively express or defend her opinions and perceived rights.*

Foreword

Three years ago, Karen and I were silently struggling in our relationship. We came from divorced families, had multiple marriages ourselves, and while we didn't know what a godly and joyful marriage looked like, we knew we didn't have one. We lived like two strangers in the same house.

When I read the first draft of this book, I laughed and I cried as I relived so much of our life through her eyes. I hadn't realized, at the time she began doing some of these things, that she was making such dramatic changes. I just noticed I was a lot happier and my love for her was growing. I was also drawing closer to God.

Husbands, I encourage you not only to get this book for your wife but read it for yourself, as well. It will help you understand the way she sees things and give you ideas to help her live in God's will. She's been exposed to many lies about what it means to be a woman, and she needs your daily prayers to help her overcome those lies. God has made you her spiritual covering, and your prayers for her are powerful. So, pray for your wife, put your trust in God, and believe in His Word. His blessings are sure to restore and enrich your marriage.

Jim Haught (2008)

The God Empowered Wife

Table of Contents

The God Empowered Wife

SECTION ONE

Preparing the Way

The God Empowered Wife

Introduction

on't worry about the details yet, but you might as well know up front: I've been married five times. I didn't know Jesus until the fifth one, and that's why we're still married. But believing in Jesus didn't make this marriage more wonderful than the others; it just made me more committed to it. The wonderful part came when I started applying biblical truth to the way I related to my husband.

You're probably wondering how a person could get married so many times. I asked myself that question a lot, too, and struggled to figure out why I kept failing at the *one thing* I wanted most of all: a happy marriage. Each of my husbands was completely different, so I couldn't blame it on choosing the same type of man each time. And *I* was always the one who left. One particularly lonely day, I realized with humility that the only thing all my husbands had in common . . . was *me*.

That was shortly into my fifth—and current—marriage; and soon afterwards, my walk with Jesus began. Seven years later, God opened a new door into my understanding of His Word; and as I applied what I learned, my marriage was transformed. I began sharing my story with other women from all over the world, and I watched in amazement as God brought about the same changes in their lives as He had in mine.

Do not conform any longer to the pattern of this world, but be transformed by the renewing of your mind (Romans 12:2).

God didn't design marriage poorly. He designed it to be one of the most incredible experiences of our lives. Yet, that's not the reality for many of us. We pride ourselves on our ability to move forward civilly after adultery, divorce, remarriage, step-parents, and half-siblings; but in the process, we've become far too pragmatic about marriage itself.

My husband has allowed me to be as transparent as possible in sharing our lives, so you can see from concrete examples that God's Word works. Some may think it was foolish to be so open; but if I'm to be a fool, then let me be a fool for Christ. I have to tell what He has done.

"I tell you," he replied, "if they keep quiet, the stones will cry out" (Luke 19:40).

This, then, is the story of my journey from doing "my best" to doing "God's best," and how the blessings that have followed exceeded my wildest dreams. Although I've chosen my words with as much care as possible for someone humbly seeking to share God's work in her life, I'm sure I've not done so perfectly. Where I have failed, I ask God to cover my errors with His Truth, so that His Word may be poured out into your life.

Karen

CB EOCB EO

1. Who Needs a Husband Anyway?

*D*oes the following sound familiar? You're efficient, smart, organized, and make sure everything that needs to get done, gets done. You're physically tired, yes, but mostly just tired of being the responsible one. Your husband is a decent guy who helps when asked—but you still have to ask, which means it's *still* your responsibility. Sometimes you joke that having a husband is like having another child.

Then, there's the marriage itself. Things look fine on the outside, but they're not really. In public, your husband is charming and cheerful. At home, he's distant or grouchy— apparently more interested in anything else than spending quality time together. Faith, instead of being something that defines your marriage, is a private, individual matter.

You've bought books on how to improve a marriage, but they all require at least some degree of cooperation from your husband. You can't make him read something he's not interested in; and learning how to be more romantic, helpful, and communicative isn't exactly high on his list.

On good days, being married is like having a roommate; on bad days it's like being in prison. Maybe that's an exaggeration, but it's a far cry from what you dreamt it would be like. With a few adjustments you could support yourself financially, and it's tempting to think life might be easier alone. The question, "Who needs a husband, anyway?" has crossed your mind more than once.

He's frustrated, too. Somewhere along the way, being married became more of a burden than a joy. The way you always "help" him drives him crazy and makes him feel inadequate. *"I don't need another mother,"* he says to himself.

You have the "right" answer for everything—at least *you* think you do—and he's tired of being corrected, criticized, and contradicted in what he says or does. It's easier to bury himself in television, hobbies, or work than fit into your world—a world where he's never quite good enough. He may not have said it out loud, but he's probably thought it: *"What does she need me for a husband, anyway?"*

 C3 80

I frequently speak with women and am always saddened to learn how many are burdened with secret heartache about their marriages. Whether they're housewives or executives; live in America, Europe, or Asia; are married to unbelievers, believers, or church leaders their sorrow is the same.

It's not just the feeling of having the world on their shoulders; it's the painful emptiness in their hearts where their husband's cherishing love and participation should have been. Most agree their husbands aren't stepping up to the plate in some way, but they don't know what to do about it. Some leave. Others try to cope.

The *martyr* keeps up a good front, even when things aren't going well. There are secrets behind her smiles, though—embarrassing secrets that she doesn't feel comfortable sharing. Some days she can barely breathe from the stress, but she remains unfailingly polite in public. Eventually, she closes off her heart to her husband. If faith is an important part of her life, she may turn to Jesus as a substitute; if not, she may turn to something else.

Then there is the *shrew*. This woman was *born* controlling other people, and marriage didn't change that. The consummate perfectionist, she resists whatever she can't control. Her temper is her most lethal weapon, and she's capable of unleashing a verbal barrage that lasts as long as she has breath or words to sustain it. Her husband, though typically easy-going, is often not as responsive to her demands and needs as she would like. When he is distant or withdrawn, she demands a resolution; and if he doesn't have one, *she* does. She's not likely to stray and neither is he; but if she rebuffs his needs too long, he may become vulnerable to temptation.

Finally, there's the *driver*. This wife satisfies the need for purpose and value that's lacking in her marriage with an activity-filled, work-filled, or child-centered life. A master of time and efficiency, she manages to accomplish more in one day than most people do in three; and while she might complain about being busy, it's really the only time she's truly happy. There's something missing in her marriage, but as long as she and her husband don't spend too much time together, they can pretend everything's fine. Of the three wives, this is the one most likely to be tempted by inappropriate relationships—and so is her husband.

Most women vacillate between these and other stereotypes, responding in self-destructive ways to the belief they're a victim of their husband's shortcomings and failings. Few have even the slightest understanding of the ability God has given them to help turn their marriage around and enjoy the deep, abiding joy He intended.

Every woman wants her husband to love her. She wants him to be faithful in his love for her and demonstrate that faithfulness with affection and respect. Even if she has a career, she wants him to be willing to provide for her.

If she's close to God—*especially* if she's close to God—she wants him to share in that closeness. In short, she wants a godly, responsible, husband who will lead her family with love.

Unfortunately, most men weren't taught how to lead a family, and many aren't certain they want to. They may have studied it in their men's groups, but there's a big difference between studying it and actually doing it—or doing it well. Even those who *are* leading aren't necessarily doing so in a godly way.

A woman can't just give her husband leadership if he isn't ready or willing to take it. On the other hand, as long as she's leading, he won't have the opportunity to learn how to *become* a godly leader. He's not likely to insist either, and why should he? She's got everything under control.

 C3 80

We may have convinced ourselves we can do marriage better than God, but the evidence proves otherwise. Our hearts are yearning, our children are struggling, and God doesn't seem to be answering our prayers. Perhaps it's because we've closed our minds to what He's already said. Why should He speak if we aren't going to listen?

> *Like the blind we grope along the wall, feeling our way like women without eyes. At midday we stumble as if it were twilight; among the strong, we are like the dead (from Isaiah 59:10).*

God has told us about submission, but it's a concept that has become so distorted we can no longer believe in it. Subservience, becoming a "nothing" to a husband's "something," or doing everything a husband wants is the false submission of the past: a secular submission that subjugates women's identity for the sake of men's glory.

Godly submission isn't weak and pandering; it's strong and confident. It doesn't disarm a woman's power and self-determination; it redirects them towards God's purposes.

My experience, as well as the experiences of other women who have implemented the ideas from this book into their lives, have convinced me—beyond doubt—that God is trustworthy and true. He can change our husbands and grow them in godliness. We just have to work *with* Him, not against Him.

03 80

So who needs a husband, anyway? Maybe you do—more than you realize. It's comparatively easy to be righteous alone. It's much harder when you have to share daily life with another person. Relationships are God's vice grips. They squeeze you until your sins ooze out—sins you wouldn't have had to face otherwise, but that enslave you and separate you from God.

If you aren't living in the peace of Christ that God promises, there's some area in your life in which you're not worshipping Him with your obedience. Chances are that area of disobedience is in your marriage. It's not all your husbands' fault, and there *is* something you can do about it.

As Gary Thomas wrote in his book, *Sacred Marriage*, "Marriage wasn't designed to make you happy; it was designed to make you holy."[1] And if you're a follower of Jesus Christ, becoming more holy is your destiny.

CB BOCB BO

Chapter 1 – Suggested Prayers

Prayer for You

Dear God,

You know things aren't right between my husband and me. You didn't design marriage to be lifeless or indifferent; but I've tried and tried to fix things on my own, and I don't know what else to do. I'm asking You to help us, and I'm willing to listen to what You have to say.

I know I can be a better wife. Show me what I may be doing wrong and what I can do differently. Help me put off a spirit of despair, frustration, and resignation, and put on a spirit of actively trusting in You.

Prepare me for Your purposes. Thank You, God. Amen.

Prayer to Give Your Husband

Dear God,

You know things aren't right between my wife and me. Grow us into the people You want us to be. Thank You, God. Amen.

Chapter 1 ~ Homework

(Begin a journal for the homework assignments)

1. Close your eyes and remember back to when you were a young girl, thinking about your future. Write about the childhood dreams you might have had for marriage. What kinds of things did you imagine?

2. As an adult, assuming a perfect marriage is possible, what would that look like to you? Focus on ways your ideas are different now than when you were a little girl.

3. How do you think your husband would describe the perfect marriage? Ask him and compare your answers.

4. How would God describe a perfect marriage? Do you agree with Him?

2. Reverse the Curse

ife was good for Adam and Eve. God said so, anyway, but the serpent convinced Eve she would be better off if she listened to her own desires. Eve chose to trust the serpent instead of God, and she convinced Adam to join her. God then cast them out of the Garden with a curse. From that point forward, they would only bring forth the fruit of their labors with pain and toil, and they would die.

At the end of His word to Eve, God added that Adam would rule over her—giving women the first of the dreaded submission clauses:

> [To Adam] *Cursed is the ground because of you; through painful toil you will eat of it all the days of your life. By the sweat of your brow you will eat your food until you return to the ground (Genesis 3:17, 19).*

> [To Eve] *I will greatly increase your pains in childbearing; with pain you will give birth to children. Your desire will be for your husband,* **and he will rule over you** *(Genesis 3:16, emphasis added).*

As modern women, we congratulate ourselves on having escaped the "curse of submission" and many of us *do* rule over our husbands. However, we also struggle mentally, physically, emotionally, and spiritually in ways we never anticipated. So, we haven't escaped the curse—we've just reversed it. We've rejected Eve's submission and ended up with Adam's toil.

On the other hand, few things rule over our thoughts and emotions as powerfully as the desire for our husbands to love us, especially when that desire is unfulfilled. Perhaps, then, we haven't escaped submission at all—we've just hidden it in our hearts. Perhaps, in our determination to be free of one "curse," we've ended up with both.

Do not be deceived: God cannot be mocked (Galatians 6:7).

We cannot go back to the kind of husband-wife relationship that denied women the rights and opportunities to which all human beings are entitled by God. What we need, instead, is a way to understand how to obey God using the personalities and strengths He has given us. We begin by looking at the culture in which we live and seeing how it has influenced who we are, today.

C3 &0

Generations ago, little boys learned how to be men by working side-by-side with their fathers to provide for their families. The industrial revolution, however, shifted the focus of men's work from family farms to factories and removed fathers from a position of daily influence in their young sons' lives.

This would have resulted in a lost generation of boys, unmentored and unsure of their place in the world, if not for the two World Wars. Military life provided the male leadership they missed growing up and gave them a practical understanding of goal-setting, self-discipline, and authority. [2]

After the wars ended, these young men exchanged their military uniforms for suits and ties and redirected their focus to business and politics. Retrospectively, they became known as "The Greatest Generation," as much for the strength of their character as for their accomplishments and impact on the shape of American institutions. [3]

On the personal front, they valued the kind of camaraderie they had known in the military. All-male clubs and bars where they could relax with their peers provided the perfect environment for socializing. Home, on the other hand, was an unfamiliar place occupied by strange people called women and children. The military had taught these men how to lead, but it had not taught them how to lead a family.

During this time, wives who had taken over the job of running the family while their husbands were at war, kept that role after the men returned—operationally at least. Actual authority reverted back to their husbands, who frequently brought military-style leadership into the home.

Single women—those who had stepped up to fill the openings in factories left by departing soldiers—had a different experience than their married sisters. The freedom of being independent and self-supporting changed their identity forever. "I'm just as capable and competent as a man!" they declared, and that realization helped birth a revolution for women.

By 1957, the Women's Liberation movement was gaining momentum, teaching girls to believe in themselves, take charge of their lives, challenge the status quo, and change the world. Fifteen years later, these girls would make "I am Woman" [4] the number one song on the Billboard chart, and its lyrics, *"I am strong, I am invincible . . . hear me roar,"* their lifelong anthem.

Ironically, it was also in 1957 that "Leave it to Beaver" first aired. As hard as it is to believe now, writers and producers of the day were conscientiously espousing traditional family values. By the early 60's, the line-up included "Father Knows Best," "The Andy Griffith Show," "The Dick Van Dyke Show," and others. Televisions were finally available in a majority of homes; and Beaver's mother, June Cleaver, soon became an icon of the traditional homemaker. The series went on to become one of the longest running shows in television history.

As a result of these diametrically opposed influences of feminism and traditionalism, young women of the era developed a curious mix of dreams and desires. They were excited about college and working . . . because it meant meeting promising men. They believed they were capable of doing anything they wanted . . . and what they wanted most of all was to find a good husband. They set out to change the world . . . with the expectation of setting aside their jobs as soon as they got married and had children.

Their newly acquired administrative and organizational skills would go with them, though, and they would begin setting business-like standards of efficiency and effectiveness in the home. Their husbands, burdened with increasing work responsibilities, would be more than happy to turn over leadership of the family to their capable wives.

These women were also the leaders of a new philosophy in child-raising, pioneered by Dr. Benjamin Spock in his book, *Baby and Child Care.*[5] Spock's philosophy was that parents didn't need outside experts to raise their children. All they needed was adequate information and a healthy respect for their children's individuality, emotions, and self-esteem.

It was a radically new idea, one well-suited to a highly educated generation, determined to do things differently than their parents—and to women who took great pride in how they managed their homes and families. Over the next sixty years, Spock's book sold more copies than any other book except the Bible. It's still the world's most popular child-raising reference.

Baby and Child Care told parents everything they needed to know about their children's physical needs but neglected to mention anything about their *spiritual* needs. In any other book, it would have been a harmless omission; however, in the "bible of parenting," it was devastating, and the impact on family life was enormous. It's not difficult, even today, to find Christian parents who avoid sharing their faith with their children for fear of "pushing" their religion on them.

By the 70's and 80's, Spock's philosophies had matured beyond their original focus on child-raising into a full-fledged, socio-cultural, self-esteem movement. In schools and families, instruction moved away from the absolute, toward a subjective understanding of feelings. "Do the right thing," children were told—not because God said so—but because it made them feel good about themselves and others. Helping children understand their emotions was not necessarily a bad thing, but indoctrinating them in the idea that feelings were a reliable compass for moral decision-making was a tragic mistake.

Spock modified a later edition of his book to include information on moral and spiritual guidance—perhaps as a result of his grandson's suicide—but it was too little, too late. By then, we were already fully engaged in worshipping the Idol of Happiness at the Temple of Self.

The heart is deceitful above all things and beyond cure (Jeremiah 17:9).

ᘓ ᘔ

The "American Dream," a term first coined in the 1930's to describe the uniquely American culture of freedom and democracy,[6] had begun changing by the late 50's into a synonym for *achieving material prosperity from humble beginnings.* For women, that meant a suburban home with all the latest appliances; 2.5 children, each with their own bedroom; 1.75 cars in the garage; and a husband with a white collar job. A family's ability to *keep up with the Jones* became the measure of its value and worth, and the race was on. Peer pressure to be successful grew exponentially.

Over the next several decades, husbands (and later, wives) worked longer and longer hours at the office and found themselves—inadvertently or not—spending more time with co-workers of the opposite sex, than with their spouses. Given a changing culture where feelings defined what was true and happiness was valued more than commitment, it was a recipe for disaster. Morality and desire collided, and morality lost. Adultery and divorce—once unspeakable tragedies—became commonplace, almost overnight.

Today, women leave their husbands as often as men leave their wives, but at the time, it was more often the latter. Women who had given up their jobs to devote their lives to their families were abandoned in record numbers for younger, more career-minded women. Often, the new wife enjoyed the financial benefits the ex-wife's sacrifices had made possible— while the ex-wife struggled to re-enter a job market where outdated office skills and "caring for family" were unacceptable applicant entries for previous work experience.

It was an irony not lost on their daughters, raised as they were in an era of feminism. These girls were greatly influenced by the sexual revolution and understood the power of assertiveness, competitiveness, and manipulation. They were attracted to young men as much as any other generation, perhaps more so, given the absence of their fathers. However, as soon as they had wooed and won their "catch," they dispensed with flirtatious pretensions and switched back to their more authoritative personality. It was time to get down to the business of having a relationship.

Their brothers, obliged to obey their mothers and respect their sisters, were often *personae non gratae* in what had become a pseudo-matriarchal environment. It wasn't easy to be a young man in a culture where "That's just like a man" was definitely not a compliment, and "Do you want to end up like your father?" was a rhetorical question. Out of sight, out of mind was the safest place to be, and keeping a low profile was the best way to avoid confrontation.

When they grew up and got married, the wives ran the family, and the husbands tried to stay out of the way. It was, after all, what they each had been raised to do.

Cʒ ꙮ

My generation was perhaps the first to set a cultural-wide precedent of wife dominance. We were defensive of our authority, but more than that, we felt we *had* to be in control in order to keep our families running smoothly. In our eyes, it wasn't really an option. Our husbands, if they were still in the picture, weren't sure how they fit in; and frankly, we weren't either.

Passionate about women's rights, we taught our daughters to reach for the stars and let nothing stand in their way. We also passed down—by example—a belief in the superiority of women and a cautious distrust of men's decision-making abilities.

As for our sons, our desire was for them to be better, kinder men than generations past. It never occurred to us to teach them how to lead a family; and if it had, it probably would have been to teach them *not* to lead. Male dominance was something we would have *discouraged,* not encouraged.

It's hard to say what effect this will have on their marriages, but it could be a moot point. Many are choosing not to get married at all.

Cʒ ꙮCʒ ꙮ

Chapter 2 - Suggested Prayers

Prayer for You

Lord,

You see my heart and know I'm not happy with the way things are in our marriage. I don't understand how my strength might be keeping my husband from being a godly leader, but I'm willing to be open-minded. Give me wisdom. Help me recognize whatever it is You want me to know and trust You enough to put it into practice.

I believe You want us to have a good marriage. Show me how to put off a spirit of worry and put on a spirit of courage and confidence to *"do what is right and not give way to fear"* *(1 Peter 3:6).* I want to be obedient so that we will have life. Thank You, Lord. Amen.

This day I call heaven and earth as witnesses against you that I have set before you life and death, blessings and curses. Now choose life, so that you and your children may live (Deuteronomy 30:19).

Prayer to Give to Your Husband

Lord,

Bless my wife and our marriage. Give us life. Thank You, Lord. Amen.

21

2 ~ Homework

1. When and where were you born? What key cultural changes
    were occurring during your formative years? What were
    your favorite television shows as a child? What did they
    teach you about men, women, and marriage?

2. What did you learn about being a wife and woman from
    your mother? Note which characteristics you sought to
    imitate and which you vowed to reject.

3. What did you learn about men and the relationship between
    husbands and wives from your father, stepfather, or other
    significant male figure?

4. How would you describe yourself as a wife (positives and
    negatives)?

5. How would you want your husband to describe you?

6. How do you think he *would* describe you if he were being
    completely honest about his feelings?

3. Searching in the Dark

I'm a product of what's known as the second wave of feminism, a time when gender equality, non-submission, and the invincibility of women so permeated girls' lives they became part of our identity without any conscious effort on our part. I'm grateful for the good things that came from feminism, but my life has been affected in many less positive ways by the delivery of that message without the balance of biblical principles.

As an adult, reading Bible verses about how wives were supposed to submit to their husbands made me nauseous. That's not an exaggeration. It wasn't that I disliked men; on the contrary, I loved them. I just didn't trust them. By then, I was also convinced they weren't as smart, capable, or hard working as women. Worse, they often lied to get what they wanted.

In contrast, my childhood dreams about men were simple and full of hope: *"When will I get married?" "What will my husband's name be?" "What will it feel like to be poised to walk down the aisle in white?"* Every man was a potential Prince Charming who might whisk me off to marital heaven, if my foot fit the glass slipper of his expectations. How we might operate as a family after getting there never crossed my mind—not once.

I had a loving, rather strict, upbringing—at least in my eyes. My Dad left my Mom for another woman around the time I started dating; and I determined Dad's preference for an independent businesswoman over his submissive, stay-at-home wife was my Mom's fault. If she hadn't been so willing to submit, he wouldn't have grown bored. There was comfort in thinking that was true: if I could avoid her mistakes, I could avoid her fate. I swore submission would never darken my life.

At the time, the right to do whatever one wanted was the answer to every question. Psychologists warned of the dangers of denying one's own happiness and exposing one's children to marital stress. Unhappy couples didn't wonder whether or not they should get divorced—they wondered whether they should do so immediately or wait until the children left home. Everyone, it seemed, was splitting up or resigning themselves to loveless marriages—a fate far worse, in my opinion.

"If I ever found myself in that situation," I vowed, *"I would chalk it up to bad judgment, get out as quickly as possible, and keep looking."* Politely, of course—no hard feelings. Having a good, loving marriage seemed more of a myth than a possibility; but I was determined to try.

I was confident of the strength of women and my own ability to accomplish whatever I set my mind to, but before I could "go boldly forth," I needed a man who loved me. The engine of my life ran on parallel railroad tracks of feminism and traditionalism. One track represented the passionate desire to find a way to make a difference *in the world.* The other represented the equally passionate desire to find a man who would make a difference *in my life.* If either was missing, I became preoccupied with trying to get it.

24

But what did a man want? Exactly what size *was* that glass slipper in his hand? Fairy tales in which handsome men sought sweet, accommodating, and beautiful women made for nice stories, but I wasn't blind. There was too much evidence in the world that putting your identity and trust in a man meant being taken for granted and abandoned. Regardless of what men *said* they wanted, it was clear what they were *attracted to* was a strong, sexy, independent woman.

Therefore, my plans for getting and keeping a husband were simple: I would be independent, yes, but also loving, pleasing, sexy, and responsible. In return, I expected my husband to be adoring, wise, generous, courteous, affectionate, careful with money, hard working, faithful, thoughtful, responsive, and kind. He would love and cherish me, appreciate my intelligence, and respect my decisions. He would never take me for granted, never treat me like a servant, never tell me what to do, and most of all, he would never, *ever* cheat on me.

With that rather primitive understanding of men and marriage—to say nothing of myself—I entered the world of dating. I thought, as most young adults do, that I was quite wise and sophisticated, with the secret formula for marriage all figured out. I was going to succeed where others had failed. *Right.*

Independent-minded and eager to be my own boss, I got an apartment at seventeen, enrolled in the university, and began working full-time to support myself. At nineteen, I graduated with honors and married the first man who asked me. The marriage was fine at first, but midway through our second year, I discovered things about him that led me to decide the marriage had been a mistake.

I aborted our child, had an affair with a married man, and filed for divorce on the newly-legal and easy grounds of "irreconcilable differences." The abortion I soon regretted. The divorce, not at all. As far as I was concerned, there was no point wasting time if he wasn't the right one.

☙ ❧

I met Husband Number Two on a blind date two months later, moved in the next week, and married him as soon as my first divorce was final. He was a wonderful husband, and we were very much in love. A great marriage, a beautiful baby son, and a bright future were all in hand by our first anniversary. I didn't think life could get any sweeter.

Then, in our sixth year, a male staff member of a church we were visiting began calling me every day. I wasn't particularly attracted to him, but his attention was flattering. If he had been blatantly flirtatious, I would have brushed it off; but he was careful not to be so obvious he couldn't deny it—which made capturing his attention all the more challenging. Before long, I couldn't get him out of my mind.

Within weeks, I started believing I had fallen out of love with my husband; and it was a short step from there into deceit, adultery, and filing for divorce, again. He didn't want to get divorced, but I couldn't figure out how to undo the damage I had already done. Even the fact that we held hands while the judge signed our decree didn't cause me to pause long enough to reconsider. It was another decision I would regret for a very long time.

A few unhappy years later, the man I had left my husband for finally asked me to marry him, and I accepted, hoping to prove I hadn't thrown away everything good and decent in my life for nothing. It was a seven-year relationship in all, marked more by tears than joy. Life had become a living hell of regret and remorse for having destroyed the family that had meant so much to me and grieving my ex-husband and son.

There was another adulterous affair—justified, I felt, by the lack of love in the marriage—and another divorce. Since I was never intimate with any of my husbands after having an affair and quickly ended each marriage, I rationalized my behavior wasn't *that* awful. By the world's definition, I was still monogamous . . . in a serial sort of way.

My son's father was eager to forgive me and take me back after each divorce, but I couldn't bring myself to agree. In spite of our wonderful memories and mutual love for our son, in spite of my burden of guilt—or perhaps *because* of it—the idea of going backwards terrified and shamed me. Reconciliation and restoration were simply not concepts I knew or understood. I just wanted to be happy.[7]

CB ED

After my third divorce, I kept moving "forward," falling for a man who sent me roses and a book of poetry after our first date—and proposed on our second. The next month, he formalized the offer on bended knee with a two-carat diamond ring. I felt like Cinderella at the ball. *Finally,* a man who could *really* provide for me and my son. Plus, he was romantic. For a woman, it doesn't get much better than that, and I wasn't about to let him get away. We married immediately.

In the coming weeks, I made what I considered to be the ultimate sacrifice for my new husband, agreeing to move nine hundred miles away from my extended family and then teenaged son, to start a new business. My son moved in with his Dad, and I convinced myself if I flew home every other weekend to see him, things would be fine.

It's amazing how easily a determined, self-justifying optimism can blind even the most passionate conscience. The single most important thing in my life had been my desire to be a good mother. Yet, it wasn't until the lights of our new city came into view that I wept from the realization I had violated even that commitment. Given my other decisions, it's not surprising I failed to grasp the magnitude of this one, too. I wanted to go back, but I had already committed to a new husband. What could I do?

CB ED

So many foolish choices, so much immorality, yet all along I was convinced I was doing the best I could. In reality, I was the North Pole of my own moral compass, wandering in circles trying to find myself. How often I wished, after I became a follower of Jesus, that someone had tried to warn me before I caused so much destruction. *"Why hadn't anyone had the courage to tell me how wrong I was?"*

I now know it was because I had avoided anyone who could, or would, tell me—and everyone else I knew was as morally lost as I was. I probably wouldn't have listened, but I might have. *"Wouldn't it have been worth the risk?"*

That's the question that haunts me now, and the reason I tell my story.

3. Searching in the Dark

Sometimes God leaves us at the mercy of our own devices and desires until we become broken enough to realize how much we need Him. Six weeks into Marriage Number Four, I discovered my new husband was a con man and everything I thought I knew about him was a lie—including the ring. When he realized I knew, he went on a two-day drunk, threatened to kill me, changed the locks and passwords at our office, and drove away. I never saw or heard from him again.

The next morning was Sunday, and going to church seemed like a reasonable thing to do under the circumstances. So, dressed in black, with everything I owned from our apartment piled in my car, I drove to the closest church and wandered the halls until I found the pastor. He was kind enough to spend a few minutes with me as I tearfully told him my fourth husband had just left me, but the poor man had no idea what to say.

Our fathers disciplined us for a little while as they thought best; but God disciplines us for our good, that we may share in his holiness (Hebrews 12:10).

The business my husband and I had started was entirely in my name, and the next morning our customers began calling to cancel their orders and request refunds. It was my intention to keep doing business as usual, but my husband had other ideas. Apparently he had called every customer—from wherever he was—and told them we were going out of business. Their deposits had already been spent on pre-production, so I couldn't have given them refunds even if I had wanted to. Unfortunately, most of them had never met me. They had only dealt with my husband.

By afternoon, lawsuits were coming in over the fax machine, employees were threatening to quit, and things were quickly spiraling out of control. For the first time in decades, I bowed my head and prayed.

> *Dear God, I need You. I'm in trouble and I don't see a way out. There is no humanly way possible for me to save myself in this situation. I don't know where else to go. Please help me.*

I had always thought of myself as a good Christian, but formal religion had disgusted me so much, I had even omitted the word "God" from my son's life to keep him free of religious hypocrisy and confusion. Personally, though, I had never stopped searching for God.

Spiritualism, new ageism, different denominations, cults, and the occult had each captured my attention in turn. I had looked everywhere for Him—everywhere, that is, except the one place where He could be found. That afternoon though, I ran straight into the arms of the God of my childhood, the God of the Bible. Somehow I knew only He had the power to help me.

Miraculously, the customers came back, the lawsuits were withdrawn, the employees stayed, and my personal safety and finances were restored. God answered my prayers so fast and so sure, any previous doubts I had about whether He was real, personal, or loving, evaporated. I may not have known Him, but He had certainly known me. He had been standing beside me all those years, just waiting for me to turn to Him.

I truly believe God answered my prayers that day, not because what I asked for was so important in the scheme of things, and certainly not because I *deserved* to have my prayers answered. I believe God answered them because He knew I would recognize it as His hand in my life, and it would open my eyes to His glory.

Just because I had found the one true God, though, didn't mean I suddenly became holy and righteous. Within weeks I was living with a new boyfriend and thinking nothing of it. God didn't force me to stop sinning, but He did give me opportunities to learn more about Him. That boyfriend, it turned out, had a huge library of taped sermons.

Night after night I listened to those tapes, reading along in my Bible and learning to pray. Cautious of being brainwashed, I critically studied and tested everything. As soon as I finished the last set of tapes, the boyfriend broke off the relationship: it had lasted just as long as it needed to—and not a day longer. God had made even my sin serve His purposes.

CB EO

I began renting a two-room suite in a widower's home and, as could be guessed, we soon started "dating." It was another case of God allowing me to suffer the consequences of my decisions, as I loaned him thousands of dollars he never repaid. God seemed to be far more interested in getting me to see the bigger picture, than in changing my immediate behavior. The transformation of my heart and my spirit would eventually take care of that.

The day before my fortieth birthday, I sat in a rocking chair by the window of my small study and randomly opened my Bible to read. It was upside down, so I inadvertently turned to Deuteronomy instead of the New Testament, but it was no accident.

This is what it said:

> *And you shall [earnestly] remember all the way which the Lord your God led you these **forty years** in the wilderness, to humble you and to prove you, to know what was in your [mind and] heart, whether you would keep His commandments or not.*
>
> *And He humbled you and allowed you to hunger and fed you with manna, which you did not know nor did your fathers know, that He might make you recognize and personally know that man does not live by bread only, but man lives by every word that proceeds out of the mouth of the Lord.*
>
> *Your clothing did not become old upon you nor did your feet swell these **forty years** (Deuteronomy 8:2-3 Amplified, emphasis added).*

I certainly hadn't known those verses were there. I hadn't even read much of the Old Testament and definitely not *that* part. I'm convinced God was telling me that my forty years of life had been a wandering in the wilderness; and that He had been there all along—watching over me, providing for me, and caring for me. He had allowed me to suffer the consequences of sin, not interfering in my foolishness or wrongdoing, in order that I might finally come to know Him and trust in His Word.

Memories I had forgotten came flooding back to my mind: the songs in Sunday school, the prayers I had written as a teen, the day I knelt in our driveway at fourteen to ask Jesus into my heart—and all the doubts and questions since then.

The rest of that chapter in Deuteronomy contained a promise that as long as God's people worshipped Him, they would be blessed. If they turned away, forgot Him as the source of their blessings, and became disobedient, He would turn away from them. It was a warning I took to heart and made my own.

It also said He was bringing His people into a land of hills and trees and streams. I didn't think much about that part until, looking back, I realized that was the week events were set in motion which would lead to my current marriage eighteen months later—and a home in the country, on a hill, surrounded by trees and streams.

It's with that marriage this story begins . . .

CR ∞

Jim leaned over the bed to give me a perfunctory kiss good-bye before he left for his early Saturday golf game. After he left, I turned on one side so I could watch out the bedroom window as he drove down the driveway and around the corner out of sight. I was used to indifference creeping into relationships; but this was my fifth marriage, and it was supposed to have been different. We weren't even to our six-month anniversary and already there was unhappiness.

The leaves on the tree outside the bedroom window fluttered gently in the breeze, and I remembered noticing that same tree the first time I had driven up his driveway. It had been our second date, and I was to meet him for breakfast on his porch before we took a drive in the country. I closed my eyes and smiled. It was a morning I could hardly have forgotten.

We had met a couple of weeks earlier and talked about how we shared a love for God, but hadn't discussed it much since then. Somehow, it felt awkward to bring it up. I really wanted to know, though—*before* I fell in love again—whether or not he truly had a heart for God.

As I had turned down the street of his neighborhood that morning, I had looked upward through the windshield, wagged a finger toward heaven, and said, *"I'm going to take my Bible in and ask him to pray with me. What do you think of that, God?"*

Normally, I wouldn't have carried a Bible in public, much less have asked a date to pray with me, and I wasn't at all sure it was okay to challenge God like that. All I knew was that I didn't want to get into another relationship unless He was in it.

Somewhat nervously, I had pulled into the long drive that arched its way up to the front of the house. By the time I reached the top of the hill, he was already walking down the porch steps to greet me—his Bible tucked under his arm. Before I could say a word, he said, "Hi, I was just reading my Bible; would you like to pray with me?" I was dumbfounded.

Despite the fact he had just separated from his wife (the divorce was drawn up, but not yet finalized) we had thrown caution to the wind, and I had moved in. Somehow, living together seemed to legitimize being physically involved.

The only unpleasant interruption of those first few months was when a workman asked how we could live "in sin," and still call ourselves Christians. *"If he only knew the whole truth,"*

I had thought, with some degree of pleasure in the face of his criticism, and making a mental note never to hire him again. It wasn't like we were murderers or anything. We were responsible, good people who loved God—and it was none of that guy's business. Nonetheless, his accusation had stuck in my mind like a burr on a sweater.

I shook my head and pulled the covers closer as if to get rid of the unpleasant memory. "Well, we're married now," I said aloud to myself. Not that being married had made much of a difference. The familiar signs of failure were already there.

God, please don't tell me this one is going to end in divorce, too. I can't fail, again. Who would have me after five divorces? Is it me? Am I doing something wrong? I've given my whole heart to each of my husbands, and it just keeps getting broken. I've even given up being with my son in order to gain their love.

Suddenly, inexplicably, the pieces all came together. It was like someone flipped on a light switch, and I could see clearly for the first time. *Only God could love me perfectly; yet I had repeatedly set aside His unfailing love to try and earn the love of men. Having paid such a huge price, I felt betrayed when they didn't meet my need for perfect love.*

Now I understood: no man could ever love me the way God could, and it was *inevitable* I would be disappointed. If I didn't let God's love fill me first, I would never be able to truly love—or be loved by—any human being.

Then and there, I fell in love with God.

When I told my husband later, he was jealous—until I explained that putting God's love first meant I no longer needed him to be perfect. I could accept him as he was, human failings and all, which meant I wouldn't be crushed when he let me down. Ironically, resting in God's love made it possible for me to love my husband *better* than before. I had heard the saying, "Put God first." Now, I understood what it meant—at least in the context of what was most important to me at the time.

> *Love the Lord your God with all your heart and with all your soul and with all your mind and with all your strength (Mark 12:30).*

There was still the Jesus thing, though. I had read in the Bible I was supposed to believe in something called the Good News, but it never seemed to say exactly what that good news was, at least not in a way I could understand. And people who talked about sin and salvation in neat, memorized clichés were never able to answer my questions logically.

"I probably have a better relationship with Jesus than they do," I thought, remembering how often I turned to Him for comfort. I didn't want to be out of God's will, but I also didn't want to take a chance on something that seemed so foolish. What if it was just made up by men?

> *The woman without the Spirit does not accept the things that come from the Spirit of God, for they are foolishness to her, and she cannot understand them, because they are spiritually discerned (from 1 Cor. 2:14).*

I couldn't stop thinking about it, though. If three years of reading and studying the Bible hadn't provided the answers I was searching for, they either didn't exist or my "holding back" had kept me from seeing them. I wanted more, but I was scared: if I started getting *weird*, could I stop?

"I can always change my mind, can't I?" I said to myself. *"Sort of like living together before getting married."* With that irreverent but comforting thought, I laid face down on my bed and stepped out into what seemed like thin air toward Jesus:

> *Dear God, I've made a mess of my life and I don't want to live this way, anymore. I don't really understand the Lord and Savior thing, but You've been there for me whenever I've needed You, and I don't want to hold back.*
>
> *Jesus, I believe You died on the cross for me, and that You are alive and living with the Father. I let go of my need to have all the answers, and I ask You to be my Lord and Savior . . . just please don't turn me into a Jesus freak. Amen.*

My prayer might not have been the most theologically elegant, but it was sincere. Over the next few weeks, I began changing, and the Bible came alive for me. When I finally grasped *why* I had needed Jesus and *what* He had saved me from, I was overwhelmed and wanted to be baptized.

> *Repent and be baptized, every one of you, in the name of Jesus Christ for the forgiveness of your sins (Acts 2:38).*

Tears were streaming down my face as I gave my testimony to the church and went under the water, but I was rejoicing as I was lifted back up. I knew I was already saved, but the water seemed to press into my physical body the decision I had made in my spirit to die to sin and live in Jesus. It was like stepping forward over a line. *I was a **new creation** in Christ; the old was gone, the new had come! (2 Cor. 5:17).*

My husband was by then a follower of Christ, too, but that's his story to tell. Naturally, since we were both believers, I expected things to look up in our marriage.

Instead, we plodded and struggled through the next five years, alternating between joy and disappointment in a determined commitment to love one another—even when we didn't. With every passing year, we grew farther apart, and I grew more confused by the growing hopelessness between us.

How long must I wrestle with my thoughts and every day have sorrow in my heart? (Psalm 13:2).

It was exactly the situation I had feared the most: "sticking it out" in a not-so-happy marriage. *"Maybe that's just the way it is, even for Christians,"* I thought; but the growing indifference between us made me wonder, *"Is being married to me really that awful?"*

I believed faith was what could restore us; yet the more I tried to share it with my husband, the more he pulled away. "You're the religious one," he would say, or "That's *your* thing, not mine." The love of God—the very thing that had first brought us together—had become our biggest stumbling block.

CB ED CB ED

Chapter 3 - Suggested Prayers

Prayer for You

Heavenly Father,

Thank you for watching over me and standing beside me in my life, even when I wasn't looking for You. I know only You can love me perfectly. Help me keep You as my first love and give me the desire to please only You. Take away any fears I might have, for You have not given me a *"spirit of timidity, but a spirit of power, of love, and of self-discipline" (2 Timothy 1:7).*

I know You want our marriage to reflect Your love, Lord. Bless our marriage and restore it. Help me rest in the knowledge that You are working in us, even now, to move us toward that goal. I praise You. I adore You. I trust You. In the Name of Jesus. Amen.

Prayer to Give to Your Husband

Heavenly Father,

Bless our marriage and restore it to a new level of love, joy, and excitement. In the Name of Jesus. Amen.

Chapter 3 ~ Homework

1. Is there any sinful decision you deeply regret having made in your life or something sinful that has happened to you that changed your life forever? In what ways do you think God might use (or already has used) those things to glorify Himself and prepare you to help others? Share with your small group.

2. What is the one prayer about yourself you most wish God would answer? Are you willing to do whatever God asks of you?

3. What is the one prayer you have *for your husband* that you most wish God would answer?

4. Memorize Mark 12:30. Write it down, along with other favorite verses that talk about the importance of loving God. Explain to someone how loving God, first, frees you to love your husband better. Note that person's name and the date in your journal.

4. Simplicity of Faith

The rest of this book is the story of how God transformed my marriage and filled it with faith, joy, and love. I'll share with you the things He revealed to me, as He revealed them, and what happened when I put them into practice—the successes *and* the failures.

As you consider these concepts for your own marriage, it's important to remember your goal must *not* be to change your husband. Your only desire must be to please God with all your heart, mind, and strength, and trust *Him* with the rest. If you don't have that in place, your efforts will be nothing more than attempts at behavioral modification. While that may effect some change, it won't transform your marriage.

God said, *"You shall have no other gods before me"* (Exodus 20:3), and that means exactly what it says. Even godly-sounding goals, like "wanting to have a good marriage" or "having a godly husband," become idols if you believe you must have them in order to be happy.[8] Put your happiness in pleasing God, first, and the rest will follow. As Jesus said, *"Seek first his kingdom and his righteousness, and all these things will be given to you as well" (Matthew 6:33).*

"I *have* been seeking God," you might say, "and nothing is changing." *Seeking God* means desiring to be in fellowship with Him—which you do by worshipping, reading the Bible, and praying. But seeking *His kingdom and His righteousness* means joining Him in His purpose—and that only comes through obedience by faith. This is what Christ embodies, and what becoming more like Christ requires.

It's not hard to know how to be obedient or pleasing to God: He tells us how in the Bible. What's hard is *wanting* to do so. We don't really trust Him with our well-being or our happiness, and why should we? In His Kingdom, the poor are rich and the rich are poor, the weak are strong and the strong are weak, children are wise and wise men are foolish—and the secret to living is dying to self.

No wonder we rely on our own intelligence instead of His. But we're never satisfied. What we think will make us happy is an illusion, and we always come up empty-handed.

> *When I surveyed all that my hands had done and what I had toiled to achieve, everything was meaningless, a chasing after the wind (Ecclesiastes 2:11).*

Worshipping God's blessings, instead of God, makes idols of those blessings. When we believe we must have something in order to be happy, we put our trust in it. True and lasting happiness, however, is found only in the fellowship of God that comes from obedience; and it is in His fellowship that we experience *all* of His blessings.

*Delight yourself in the LORD and he will give you
the desires of your heart (Psalm 37:4).*

☙ ❧

I'll admit the phrase, *"Helping your husband become a
godly leader,"* was deliberately construed to appeal to your
human, self-pleasing nature. Consider it now as a reminder and
a promise that when you, as a wife, consciously and actively
seek to please God in faith, He will move in your husband. You
don't change him, God does.

Letting go of trying to bring about change through your
own efforts is hard. It requires trusting God and His power to
bring about what He intends, more than you trust yourself. In
order to obey, you have to trust; and in order to trust, you must
first believe.

There are so many people today who are like I was,
calling themselves Christians, but not confidently believing and
trusting in Him, I want to make sure we're all on the same page.
It's not possible to have the marriage God has planned for
you—and you desire—in your own strength. You have to have
Jesus, so we'll start with Him.

The rest of this chapter is a compilation of various online
conversations I've had with people—some Christian and some
not—who've expressed common doubts about Christ and
Christianity. I've used the initials KB to represent myself, and
PS to represent the other person, because there always seems to
be "one more" question.

☙ ❧

The God Empowered Wife

PS: Jesus was a socialist magician who was just a nice guy. You need to open your mind a little bit more. Live dangerously, it's FUN! There is more to life than "believer and "non-believer," right and wrong.

KB: You don't know fun until you know what it's like to live with the Creator of the universe moving through you. You can't get there on your own.

PS: I don't think you have enough faith in yourself if you don't think you can get there on your own.

KB: You're right. I don't have enough faith in myself. I can't even keep my own New Year's resolutions. If reaching God depends on me, I'm in trouble.

PS: You do talk sense, but Christianity starts to fail when it talks about this all-powerful, personal god. If God's so powerful, why does He let bad things happen? Why doesn't He get rid of evil?

KB: Someday He will. *"The Son of Man will send out his angels, and weed out everything that causes sin and all who do evil" (Matthew 13:4).*

PS: Why not now?

KB: All right, you get your wish. Tonight's the night God's going to destroy all evil. Whom should He start with?

PS: Hmmm. I don't know.

KB: It's something to think about. Let's say, hypothetically, you and someone else were acting evilly toward each other, and God destroyed the other person first. As soon as

44

He did that, you wouldn't have a reason to act evilly anymore, so should God still destroy you, or not?

PS: I see what you mean.

KB: It kind of begs the question whether God should consider past evil, present evil, or *potential* evil, doesn't it?

PS: I guess all three.

KB: Imagine facing God, with all your potential for sin and evil laid bare. Now, there's a scary thought. By the way, whose definition of sin and evil should He use—yours or your enemy's?

PS: Is that a trick question?

KB: No. Your enemy is evil in your eyes, and you're evil in your enemy's eyes, so it does matter.

PS: So what's the answer?

KB: He uses His *own* definition of sin and evil, which—in case you were wondering—is in the Bible.

PS: I don't read the Bible much.

KB: How will you know how you measure up against His definition of evil, then, when He destroys all that evil you want destroyed?

CS &

PS: Just because I've done some bad things in my life, doesn't mean I'm evil.

KB: Even a murderer says she's not evil. What makes you so different?

PS: Well, maybe she was just raised in a really bad situation. Is it her fault? I mean, I might even murder someone if I had been raised in her circumstances.

KB: So given the right circumstances, you could see yourself doing something really evil?

PS: Sure.

KB: Then is it fair for God to treat you differently than a murderer, just because you were raised in better circumstances? If anything, He should be harder on you since you had everything in your favor.

PS: I hadn't thought of it that way before.

CS ✂️

PS: How do you know following Jesus is right? Maybe you're thinking you're devout, but really you're making God hate you more every day for believing the wrong thing.

KB: Let me make sure I've got this right. You're saying if a person believes in the wrong thing—even if they believe it with all their heart—if it's wrong, God will still be angry?

PS: Yeah.

KB: Like, even if you don't believe in gravity, when you step off the edge of a cliff, you're still going fall, right?

PS: Exactly.

KB: It's pretty important to make sure you're trusting in the right thing, then.

PS: I see where you're going. When it comes to religions, I don't agree. I think they're all just different paths to the same mountaintop, so to speak.

KB: Whether they are or they aren't, the next question is still the same: How do you get to that destination, that mountaintop as you call it, in each of those religions?

PS: You just follow the rules of that religion, whatever you're supposed to do.

KB: What if you don't meet all those rules perfectly?

PS: I guess you don't get to where you want to go.

KB: How many perfect Christians have you known? I don't mean Jesus, who was a Jew anyway. I mean regular people.

PS: None.

KB: How many perfect Jews or Muslims can you think of?

PS: None.

KB: Know a perfect Buddhist, Hindu, atheist, or agnostic?

PS: No. None.

KB: Can you think of *anyone* who is perfect? Are *you* capable of being perfect?

PS: No.

KB: So how do you get to the "top of the mountain" then?

PS: I don't know. Maybe you just have to be a good person.

⊂3 ∞

KB: Do you consider yourself a good person?[9]

PS: Yeah. I'm not perfect, but I'm a good person.

KB: Have you ever lied?

PS: Sure.

KB: So what does that make you?

PS: A liar.

KB: Have you ever taken something that's not yours?

PS: No.

KB: Are you sure? You just told me you're a liar.

PS: Well, okay. Yes.

KB: What does that make you?

PS: Someone who steals. I guess a thief.

KB: Have you ever used God's name as a curse word?

PS: Who hasn't?

KB: Would you use your mom's name as a curse word?

PS: Well, no.

KB: You wouldn't use your mom's name as a curse word, but you use God's name. That's blasphemy.

PS: It's just something everybody does. It's a cultural thing.

KB: What about looking at someone other than your husband, with lust—which is adultery of the heart; or being angry at someone, which Jesus says is the same as murdering them in your heart? Ever been guilty of those?

PS: Of course.

KB: Then, in your heart you're a lying, thieving, blasphemous, adulterous, murderer. If you had to stand before God, would you be innocent or guilty?

PS: Obviously, guilty. I still think I'd go to heaven, though. If there's a God, I believe He's loving and good.

KB: If you were in a regular courtroom, accused of a crime, and said, "Judge, I know you're a fair and decent man, so even though I'm guilty—and I admit I am—will you forgive me and let me go free?" He'd probably say, "Yes, I am fair and decent, which is why I have to make sure justice is done." Then he would give you a just punishment. A good judge doesn't let the guilty go free.

PS: Doesn't God weigh the good things I've done, against the bad? [10]

KB: Interesting question. Think of five really good people and five really bad people, then write them down from best to worst and include yourself in the list.

PS: Okay.

KB: Now, draw a dividing line that shows the pass/fail point separating people whose good works outnumber their bad ones, from those whose bad works outnumber their good.

PS: Got it.

KB: Did you put yourself in the middle, slightly on the "good" side?

PS: How did you know?

KB: *"Worse than some, better than most."* That's the way most people describe themselves. Even people you might call evil—like the ones you put on the "bad" side of your chart.

PS: So where *is* the dividing line, then?

KB: *"Whoever keeps the whole law and yet stumbles at just one point is guilty of breaking all of it" (James 2:10).*

PS: So everyone fails?

KB: *"No one is good but God alone" (Luke 18:19).*

PS: Well, great. If no one's good and God's so all-powerful, why doesn't He just figure out a way to get rid of the evil in us, and make us all okay, *without* destroying us?

KB: He did, He provided Jesus, the *"Lamb of God, who takes away the sin of the world" (John 1:29).*

PS: That's just way too exclusive and self-righteous for me.

KB: Really? It says "the sin of the *world.*" A little later in the Bible, it says, *"For God so loved the world that he gave his one and only Son, that whoever believes in him shall not perish but have eternal life" (John 3:16).*

PS: I've heard that a hundred times.

KB: Then listen to it closely. *"Whoever believes"* means anyone who believes, and *"the world"* means, well, the world. It doesn't get much more inclusive than that. Other religions—ones that require you to do something on your own to get to God are the exclusive ones. They exclude even their own if they don't measure up.

PS: It makes more sense to me that everyone just keeps coming back in different lives, doing things over and over, and learning until they get it right.

KB: That's still your own effort. Why would you want to keep suffering if Jesus is willing and ready to give you godly wisdom, pay the price for your sin, and set you free, right now—just by asking?

PS: I don't know.

CB EO

There were two thieves crucified at the same time Jesus was. One was defiant and mocked Jesus: *"Aren't you the Christ? Save yourself and us!" (Luke 23:39).*

The other thief may not have understood why Jesus had to be crucified, but he knew He was innocent. This thief recognized the difference between himself, a sinner who deserved to be punished, and Jesus, who was holy. He chastised the first thief.

"We are punished justly, for we are getting what our deeds deserve. But this man has done nothing wrong" (Luke 23:41). Then he asked Jesus, *"Remember me when you come into your kingdom" (Luke 23:42).*

Jesus replied, *"Today you will be with me in paradise" (Luke 23:43).*

Jesus knew the man was a thief, not one of His followers. He didn't ask if he had prayed every day or followed the law. He just saw his repentant, believing, desiring heart, and welcomed him into His presence for eternity.

For my Father's will is that everyone who looks to the Son and believes in him shall have eternal life, and I will raise him up at the last day (John 6:40).

CB 80

PS: I think I'm getting the picture.

KB: Don't take my word for it. Examine your heart. Ask God to give you wisdom and show you the truth. He will.

PS: And then what?

KB: Make your life count. Turn away from your old way of thinking and turn toward Jesus. *"Confess with your mouth, 'Jesus is Lord,' and believe in your heart that God raised him from the dead, and you will be saved. For it is with your heart that you believe and are justified, and it is with your mouth that you confess and are saved.*

"As the Scripture says, 'Anyone who trusts in him will never be put to shame.' . . . The same Lord is Lord of all and richly blesses all who call on him, for, 'everyone who calls on the name of the Lord will be saved'" (from Romans 10:9-13).

CB 80CB 80

Chapter 4 ~ Suggested Prayers

Prayer for You – A Prayer of Faith

Heavenly Father,

I always thought You wanted me to be a good person. Now I understand only You are good and I can never be good enough on my own. You are the one true God, and by my sin, I am separated from you. Thank you that through Jesus, I can be made perfect in Your eyes. I believe He lived and died and is alive again—proof He has overcome sin and death. I believe He can separate me from my sin and reconcile me to You. I believe, through Him, that I am forgiven.

I reject my sin and put my trust now in Jesus to be my Lord and Savior. Fill me with the Holy Spirit to teach me about Your heart, and fill me with the joy and peace of knowing You.

Jesus, I'm ready to take Your hand, leave behind my sin and the way I've been living, die to myself, and become a new person in You. I will love you with *"all my heart, all my soul, all my strength, and all my mind" (Luke 10:27).* Make it my greatest desire and my deepest joy to walk in Your ways. Amen.

Prayer to Give to Your Husband

Heavenly Father,

Thank you for my wife and for her faith in You. Help me see her through Your eyes and love her because she is Your child. Draw us near to You. In the Name of Jesus. Amen.

Chapter 4 ~ Homework

1. How would you convince a skeptical stranger that your child is really yours? Conversely, how would your child convince a skeptical stranger that you really are his or her parent? Try to think of five evidences or proofs for each.

2. How would you convince a skeptical stranger that you are really *a child of God* belonging to Christ? List five credible evidences. Look at the Gospel of John and identify verses that point to evidence.

3. Memorize John 1:12-13. Ask God to give you at least one opportunity this week to explain that verse to someone who doesn't know it. Write down their name and the situation.

4. Every day, all over the world, followers of Jesus are beaten, imprisoned, or killed for their faith. Visit some of the websites listed below and sign up for a newsletter. The next time you pray, imagine you are wasting away in a cold, dark cell, sore from torture or beating, separated from your family for years—simply because you wouldn't abandon your faith. What is it about having so much freedom and material goods that makes it hard for us to grasp this kind of faith for ourselves? Read and discuss Matthew 5:1-10 and 19:21-24 in light of these thoughts.

www.opendoorsusa.org
www.secretbelievers.org
www.persecution.com

SECTION TWO

Getting Started

5. No Man Can Serve Two Masters

*I*t was hot in Africa in June. I had come to the country of Cameroon on business; but since my host was a follower of Jesus, we passed the time between meetings trying to escape the heat and discussing Christian life. One morning, we were standing in the shade of a concrete building, waiting for our driver to arrive.

"You suggested," he began hesitantly, "that I ask my wife what she would like me to pray for her." He looked down at his shoes, but I could see there were tears in his eyes. "She said," he continued, "the most important thing I could pray for her was for *me* to be a godly man and leader for our family."

The car arrived, and as we rode to the meeting I thought about what he had said. There I was, halfway across the world, and his wife's request was *word-for-word* the same as what women I knew back home were praying. Only a few months earlier I had understood my own longing in this area . . .

ଓ ଃ

The men in our church had gathered on stage one Sunday, to commemorate the completion of a church-wide men's Bible study. We had known they would be singing, but we hadn't known what song. The lights dimmed, and their four hundred voices began to fill the sanctuary:

> *Come and fill our homes with Your presence,*
> *You alone are worthy of our rev'rence.*
> *As for me and my house, we will serve the Lord.*

These were our husbands, just regular guys who aggravated us and sometimes let us down; but in that moment, they seemed different. They seemed like men of God.

> *We vow to live holy, bowing our knees to You only.*
> *Staying together, praying together,*
> *Any storm we can weather, trusting in God's Word.*
> *As for me and my house, we will serve the Lord.* [11]

Rising to my feet to honor my husband, I became aware of how much I *liked* seeing him in this new light. I realized then that I wanted him to be the godly leader of our family; I just didn't know why he *wasn't,* or how he could ever get there. Most of all, I didn't have any idea how I was standing in the way of that ever happening.

CB ♡

Later, I opened my Bible to the fifth chapter of Ephesians, trying to figure out what I was supposed to do with these new thoughts. The idea of husband leadership fell dangerously close to wife submission, and that was one area of scripture I had deliberately avoided—or at least read over quickly and dismissed as irrelevant in our modern era. This time, it was like God was speaking directly to me:

"Wives, submit to your husbands as to the Lord. For the husband is the head of the wife as Christ is the head of the church, his body, of which he is the Savior" (Ephesians 5:22-24).

"Submission is the root cause of everything that is, and ever has been, wrong with marriage," I protested. "I don't see how I can reconcile that with what You're saying."

"There is a way that seems right to a woman, but in the end it leads to death" (from Proverbs 14:12).

"Even if I wanted to submit, I couldn't. It's too hard."

"What I am commanding you today is not too difficult for you or beyond your reach" (Deuteronomy 30:11).

"But Lord, I tried it in the past, and he didn't like it. He said he married me because I am strong and confident; he doesn't want me to be sweet and doting. Since that verse was obviously written for him and he doesn't care if I obey it or not, then even if I'm being disobedient, it's disobedience by mutual agreement. Isn't that okay?"

"Why do you call me, 'Lord, Lord,' and do not do what I say?" (Luke 6:46).

"It's impossible, Lord! I'm not meek and quiet, and I don't even know how *not* to have dreams and aspirations. Why would You want me to deny who I am and try to be someone I'm not?"

"What is impossible with men is possible with God" (Luke 18:27).

At that moment, the Holy Spirit revealed to me the problem wasn't just that I was uncomfortable with the idea of being submissive. My husband was uncomfortable with the idea of leading, too. That surprised me. How could *my* husband—a retired Army Colonel, former CEO of private and public companies, a natural born leader, the guy who always rises to the top—not be comfortable leading?

The more I thought about it, though, the more it made sense. I took care of everything. I made all the decisions, and he not only let me—he asked me to. As my resistance began to soften, another verse came to mind:

No one can serve two masters; for either he will hate the one and love the other, or he will be devoted to one and despise the other (Matthew 6:24).

One of my greatest heartaches over the years had been the way my husband seemed to have lost his love for the Lord. He could hide it well in church, but I knew better. That verse, which I had previously thought of only with regard to putting my trust in money instead of God, now made sense to me in a new way.

If I was the master of our family, then I was the master of my husband, and that verse said he would be serving me—not God. He would even hate God, or me, and I had seen evidence of both of those. I thought about that for a minute.

Maybe God didn't give wives those commands about submitting to husbands because He thinks we are less wise, less strong, or less godly than they are. Maybe He gave them to us because we are so strong and so wise and so close to God that when we take over, we don't leave room for our husbands to grow in their own strength and wisdom and godliness.

If that was right, then all the time I had been asking God to change my husband, I had been resisting the very instrument he would use to accomplish that change—*the role of leader.* The concept of submission might have been too difficult for me to embrace, but the idea of getting out of the way and giving my husband opportunities to lead seemed challenging and interesting. It was something *to do*, not just something *to be*. It had power and purpose.

That change of perception was so simple, yet so profound, it was as if, in that instant, my life stopped rotating in one direction and slowly started rotating in the other.

ርዝ ຂວርዝ ຂວ

Chapter 5 ~ Suggested Prayers

Prayer for You

Dear God,

I confess I haven't been obedient to you in every way I could have been. I admit I've been afraid. But You've always been faithful to give me strength and help me trust in You. I need strength now, for a new thing. Show me where I have become the master of our family.

Bless my husband, Lord. I know what You are doing in him is between the two of you, and I can't be his Holy Spirit; but I pray that as I step out of the way, He will be drawn closer to You and hear Your voice.

May we both focus on pleasing You, not on pleasing each other or ourselves, confident that with the one will come the other. Bless our marriage and be with us as we grow. In the Name of Jesus. Amen.

Prayer to Give to Your Husband

Dear God,

I'm thankful You gave me my wife. Show me how to please You in being the leader of our family that You want me to be, so she can be the wife You want her to be. In the Name of Jesus. Amen.

Chapter 5 - Homework

1. Ask your husband to give you some examples of when you are bossy to him. If he hesitates, ask him to let you know when you are *being* bossy. If he still hesitates or denies you are bossy, ask someone who regularly observes you with your husband—for example, a child, relative, or friend.

2. In what areas of your marriage do you make most of the decisions? Next to each, note whether you took on that responsibility because you wanted to, or because your husband wouldn't (or didn't).

3. Memorize Matthew 6:24. Explain to at least one person how that verse applies to wives being the master of the family. Write the names of those you shared it with.

4. What one thing would prove to you that God was blessing your obedience as you faithfully practice letting your husband lead over the next year or two? Be specific.

6. Active Submission

There are many ungodly forms of submission. My husband's father, for example, was a good man, but he used his position as leader of the family to treat his wife like a servant. His idea of being "master of the house" was to have his wife wait on him hand and foot while he sat in his easy chair. That's servitude, not submission; and it helps husbands become self-centered and *un*godly.

Like many women of her generation, his wife responded as kindly and obediently as she could. She knew in her heart it wasn't right, but she didn't know how to help him be a godly leader, instead. When we were alone, she warned me not to let my husband follow in his father's footsteps. It was a warning I needed little urging to heed.

Another type of ungodly submission demands subservience in thought and doesn't allow a wife to participate in decisions for the family. This also is not godly submission, but a violation of God's commands for husbands to treat their wives as equal heirs in Christ.

A third version involves treating women like property or animals, inferior to men, with minimum rights. In this way of thinking, women can be denied their freedom and even beaten or killed for not obeying their husbands.

None of these are godly forms of submission, but distortions created by men to elevate themselves to the position of gods. Yet we women are guilty of perpetuating an equally ungodly type of submission: husband submission.

We emasculate our husbands by mothering them and then complain they aren't stepping up to the plate. When that doesn't work, we use thinly disguised attempts to control and change them—pushing and prodding them to do what we think they should, or setting a "good example" and hoping they'll get the hint. Eventually, we end up way out in front, stretched thin trying to pull our husbands forward and wondering why they aren't cooperating. It's like trying to pull an animal that doesn't want to budge. We become the dominant spouse, even if that wasn't our original intent.

The problem is, men weren't designed to follow women, at least not when it comes to learning how to be a man. Even the lowliest man has a God-given need to lead his family, and when he can't—or won't—he isn't fulfilling the purpose for which he was created. He will likely become depressed, withdrawn, or angry, and turn to other things or people to fill that need and purpose. It's not what he really wants, but he doesn't know how to lead in a way that his wife will follow. And his wife doesn't know how to follow a man who isn't leading in a godly way.

"I've *tried* submission before," you may be saying, "and it didn't work." You probably waited until a situation came up that you and your husband disagreed on; then, torn between what you knew was best for the family or submitting to him, you gave in. In other words, you went about business as usual and picked the worst possible time to let him take the lead: an important decision you were certain he was wrong about. There were bound to be problems.

Or you might have decided you were going to "turn over a new leaf" and try to be meek and passive. That didn't last long, either. You could no more be a meek and passive woman than a tree could be a blade of grass, and your husband wouldn't want you to be. He married you because he's attracted to your strength. What pride could he take in leading someone who's a wimp?

Another ineffective, though well-intentioned, type of false submission is trying to proactively meet your husband's needs *before* he knows what those needs are—or before he's decided he even wants your help. Not only does that usually mean you are more focused on pleasing him than on pleasing God, it also denies your husband the opportunity to realize just how much he really *does* need you. Consequently, even if he appreciates your efforts, it still feels like meddling to him—and in a way, it is.

You're only doing it because you care, but it backfires and this is why: taking the initiative to solve your husband's problems before he has asked for help is actually a subtle form of control. Only *he* knows what is in his own heart, and you should wait and listen, trusting him to tell you when he wants you to get involved. By preempting his requests, you imply you know what he needs better than he does—which is just another form of domination and mothering disguised as submission.

Cß ßÐ

Saying you'll "be submissive" is a passive putting-off of dominant behavior. It's a resolution, and resolutions are merely an *intention* to do something differently. You must actively replace the old behavior with a new, godly one, or the resolution won't stick. You'll go right back to your old behavior, and the situation will be worse than it was before.

> *When an evil spirit comes out of a woman, it goes through arid places seeking rest and does not find it. Then it says, "I will return to the house I left." When it arrives, it finds the house unoccupied, swept clean and put in order.*
>
> *Then it goes and takes with it seven other spirits more wicked than itself, and they go in and live there. And the final condition of that woman is worse than the first. That is how it will be with this wicked generation (from Matthew 12:43-45).*

In other words, simply deciding you're going to be submissive is *not* godly submission. At some point, your dominant spirit will return, bringing with it the seven spirits that accompany broken resolutions: disappointment, guilt, blame, anger, self-righteousness, hard-heartedness, resentment, and rejection of God's Word.

You can't just stop doing something that's wrong; you have to start doing something right in its place. A thief doesn't stop being a thief when she decides to stop stealing: she stops being a thief when she starts working and giving. Similarly, you don't stop being dominant when you decide to stop telling your husband what to do. You stop being dominant when you start creating *opportunities* for him to lead.

*You were taught, with regard to your former way of life, to **put off your old self**, which is being corrupted by its deceitful desires; to be made new in the attitude of your minds; and to **put on the new self**, created to be like God in true righteousness and holiness (Ephesians 4:22-24, emphasis added).*

Here's another way of looking at it: you wouldn't say an apple tree was no longer an apple tree just because all the apples had fallen off. You would only say it wasn't an apple tree if you found something new, like a peach, growing on it. Similarly, you don't stop being the leader of the family when you stop being dominant; you stop being the leader when you start actively creating opportunities for your husband to lead. That's **Active Submission.**

A tree is recognized by its fruit (Matthew 12:33b).

℃ ℅

Generally speaking, men fear failure; so if your husband has not been leading, he's not likely to take the initiative now, no matter how often you tell him he should. On the other hand, he can't take leadership without your permission or he becomes a dictator. True leadership can never be taken; it can only be given by someone willing to follow.

Therefore, the *first* step in Active Submission is to mentally put yourself in the position of follower behind your husband, rather than trying to get him to step up to the plate as a godly leader. In so doing, you put him in the *position* of leadership, without requiring him to earn it or prove himself worthy of it. And it's in the position of leadership that God will bring about the very changes He has planned for him.

The *second* part of Active Submission is to watch for opportunities to let your husband practice leading. Figuratively speaking, all you really have to do is wait. Sooner or later, he'll take a step forward, and when you move forward with him— voilà—he's leading. He probably won't even realize it at first because he's not doing anything different than usual; he's only leading because you're following.

If you want to speed things up a little, and I'm sure you will, you can start looking for ways to create additional opportunities for him to practice and strengthen his leadership skills and decision-making abilities. These **Moments of Leadership** should be low-risk, low-emotion, situations in which you feel safe taking a step back and inviting him to lead, without worrying about the results.

Remember, whether or not your husband steps into the opportunities you create for him is between him and God. It's none of your business. The minute you become emotionally invested in the results, you have started trying to be the coach and quarterback for your husband's life—roles which belong only to God.

Be on guard for the tell-tale signs of thinking or telling your husband what he should do. No matter how diplomatic you are, you're still trying to be his conscience and play Holy Spirit, which never works. Your husband will tune you out; and when his conscience or the Holy Spirit actually does speak to him, he'll think he's hearing your voice again and tune them out, too.

The *third* step in Active Submission is realizing that one of your husband's greatest fulfillments will come from being a godly man, and one of your greatest joys will come from being married to one. So look for ways to help him become, not just any leader, but a *godly* leader. You don't do this by teaching your husband how to lead or trying to solve his problems, but by pointing him to God for answers.

Offer your thoughts, if you must, and let him know you will be praying for him, but resist the impulse to jump in and give advice unless he specifically asks for your help—then do so sparingly. Don't guide him, don't push him, and don't judge him. If he falls backward, support him with your love and prayers, and let him get back up on his own. Remember, he's a man. Don't treat him like a child.

He may turn to you for advice when he's unsure, hoping you'll take over, but keep encouraging him to look to God. Difficulties are opportunities to grow in our understanding of our relationship to God, and you deprive your husband of that blessing when you try to solve his problems for him. That's not to say God can't work through you to help your husband, but use careful discretion and don't let fear motivate you into taking control.

Active Submission is not about being a doormat; it's about being a firm and supporting foundation. In a strange way, it reveals your *real* power and wisdom: the power to give or take away your husband's leadership by your willingness to follow him, and the wisdom to let him experience God—on God's timetable, not yours.

Cʒ ৪০

The next seven chapters in this book give examples of Moments of Leadership and Active Submission that are so subtle your husband probably won't realize you're doing them. He'll just notice he's happier in the relationship, and you'll notice he's growing in godliness. If he isn't, check *your* heart, not his. Are you trying to please God, or are you trying to change your husband?

We make it our goal to please God, whether we are
at home in the body or away from it (2 Cor. 5:9).

Give yourself at least a week to practice each one. They're pretty much fail-safe because you aren't setting expectations, and you aren't asking your husband to do anything he isn't already doing. You're just creating opportunities for him to lead, so you can follow. When you notice him slipping back into his old ways, examine yourself. Chances are you've slipped back into dominating behavior. Control and manipulation wear many clever disguises.

Learning to give your husband opportunities to lead is a skill, and learning a new skill isn't easy. You have to practice to master it, and then you have to keep practicing to maintain and improve it. No one expects a first-year musician or golfer to play well—or a pro to *keep* doing well—without practice. Neither should you expect to master Active Submission, or your husband to master being a godly leader, overnight. Be patient in perseverance as God grows you both.

Perseverance must finish its work so that you may
be mature and complete, not lacking anything (James
1:4).

Since your husband isn't accustomed to leading the family in a godly way, don't suddenly give him the reins in every area. That would be like throwing four hundred pound barbells on a man who hasn't developed the muscle strength to lift them. Instead, start with lighter weights—decisions that have less risk—and build up to tougher decisions as he gains confidence in his skills and you gain confidence in his wisdom. That's what it means to give him Moments of Leadership.

Finally, remember that every moment of your life is a potential act of worship. In each situation, you have a decision to make: will you try to please yourself, your husband, or God? What you answer reveals whom you have chosen to worship.

CR ꝏ

Before going on, let's review the steps of Active Submission:

First, commit to a change of heart by repositioning yourself mentally from leading your husband, to following him.

Second, look for low-risk, low-emotion opportunities to create Moments of Leadership.

Third, help him stay focused on pleasing God, instead of on pleasing himself or you.

Once your husband realizes he's actually leading, he'll look over his shoulder now and then to see if you're really there. When he sees you are, he'll step forward; and before long, you'll start seeing more faith in his spirit, love in his heart, pride in his step, and an increasing desire to provide and care for you. Isn't that what you've been praying for?

CR ꝏCR ꝏ

Chapter 6 - Suggested Prayers

Prayer for You

Dear Lord,

Help me look for ways to step back and let my husband lead. Remind me that my goal is not to change him, to get him to do what I want, or even to "try to be submissive." My only goal is to be pleasing to You.

With your help, I am going to put off dominant behavior and begin to actively help my husband become a godly leader by looking for opportunities to let him lead. When I falter, remind me that my greatest joy will come from pleasing You. Bless my efforts and give me hope to persevere.

I commit to using the strength and intelligence You have given me to honor You and Your Word. Bless my husband and give him wisdom and discernment to lead well. In the Name of Jesus Christ. Amen.

Prayer to Give to Your Husband

Dear Lord,

Thank you for giving my wife gifts of strength and intelligence. Help me lead my family well, so she will trust and respect me, and together we might be pleasing to You. In the Name of Jesus Christ. Amen.

Chapter 6 ~ Homework

1. Close your eyes and think of the things that have bothered you the most about your husband. Is your face frowning, pinched, serious? List the things you were thinking.

2. Now, think back to when you first met your husband and the things that attracted you to him. How did your face change? Note your observations and what you were thinking.

3. This week, when you're tempted to fret about your husband, smile and ask God to bless the work of his hands and his leadership efforts. Notice how hard it is to pray anxious or complaining prayers when you're smiling.

4. Memorize 2 Corinthians 5:9. Share it with three people, in a life application. Write down their names and the situations.

5. Write a definition for Active Submission, comparing it to how you used to think of submission. Check your definition by looking back in this chapter.

The God Empowered Wife

76

7. Moments of Leadership

When I told my husband I had made a commitment to obey God in the area of submission, he raised an eyebrow and snickered as if to say, *"Yeah, right."* He had grown accustomed to expecting argument, correction, and having my decisions forced on him. I guess he didn't think I would, or could, change. When he told his men's small group, they weren't so polite. They laughed out loud.

In spite of such an inauspicious beginning, I was determined. The first thing I wondered was, *"How do I give my husband a low-risk, frequent opportunity to practice leading when he's not even interested in leading?"* The only thing I could think of were the conversations we had about what to do in the evening. They usually went something like this:

Him: "What do you want to do tonight?"

Me: *(Not having thought about it)* "I'm not sure."

Him: "Let's go out to eat."

Me: *(Not wanting to pay good money to just stare at each other)* "No, let's go to a movie."

Him: "OK. You pick it."

Me: *(Resisting)* "No, you pick it."

Him: "Adventures of the Warrior."
Me: "Ugh . . . how about, 'In Love' instead?"
Him: *(Sighing)* "Whatever."
Me: *(Feeling guilty, wanting to be nice, and thinking about the calories in buttered popcorn)* "You know what, let's just eat out."
Him: "No, the movie is fine."
Me: "No, really, we should eat out."
Him: "Where, then?"
Me: "Anywhere. How about Italian?"
Him: "How about Mexican."
Me: *(Calculating the calories in Mexican food vs. those in popcorn)* "Let's just go to the movies after all. We can eat popcorn and skip dinner."
Him: *(Coolly, not really wanting to do anything anymore)* "Fine, let's just go."

Notice that no matter what my husband suggested, a different idea always popped into my head that seemed better. I wasn't trying to be obnoxious; it just happened. Being the good-natured guy he was, he gave in, which made me—by default—the decision-maker.

It seemed like a good place to turn the tables and give him the decision-making leadership role. All I had to do was agree to his ideas, instead of trying to "improve" them. Now the conversation went like this:

Him: "What do you want to do tonight?"
Me: *(Not having thought about it yet)* "I'm not sure.
Him: "Let's go out to eat."

Me: "Okay!"
Him: "Where do you want to go?"
Me: "How about Italian?"
Him: "Mmm...Mexican"
Me: "Sure. Sounds great."
Him: *(Warmly)* "Great! Let's go."

It was amazing what a difference that simple little change made. We both started enjoying our evenings together, and he even planned some for us on his own. It was like being on a date. You might think I was denying myself, but it didn't feel that way at all. It was actually a lot of fun to see how quickly he started looking forward to going out with me.

I don't want to belabor the point, but it's important to note if my heart hadn't been in the right place, my agreeableness would have seemed contrived. I wasn't thinking, *"If I say this, then he'll say that."* I was thinking, *"How can I let my husband lead in this situation, in a way that is pleasing to God?"*

There were definitely benefits to going along with what my husband already wanted to do, rather than trying to get him to do what *I* thought he should want to do. It was easier, for one thing, and more fun. His decisions might not have been as efficient or as economical as mine, but who cared? He wanted to go out with me. All that inner dialogue and worry about making the "right" decision had been a noble cause, but I had been sacrificing my marriage to it.

There was only one time I *really* didn't want to go where he wanted and "submission resentment" crept in. I tried to think of ways I could offer a different idea without taking the lead, but nothing came to mind; so I gritted my teeth, smiled, and said, "Sure, let's go." I dreaded the meal but was curious to see what would come of trying to please God, instead of myself.

I don't know if my husband was right about it being a wonderful restaurant, or if God just blessed my obedience, but we had a great time. We talked and laughed, he was sweet and attentive, and it became one of my favorite places. I learned a valuable lesson that night: I really *don't* know everything—even about myself.

CB ED

One afternoon, as we were shopping together, I decided to practice Moments of Leadership by asking him what brand or size of grocery items he thought we should get. I know that sounds silly, but what better place to give him opportunities to lead in low-risk, frequent decisions?

I was shocked when I realized that no matter *what* he suggested, I immediately thought of why some other brand or size would be better. It was as though, by virtue of it having been his suggestion, I automatically rejected it. Fortunately, I kept my mouth shut, but it was humbling to see how much self-righteousness was buried in my heart.

Set a guard over my mouth, O LORD; keep watch over the door of my lips (Psalm 141:3).

I'm not saying I *always* agree with my husband or *never* recommend something I want to do, but he has become so much more loving that the joy I get from agreeing to his suggestions goes well beyond the decision at hand. Of course, if he were to suggest something sinful, I would refuse. It's not likely he would, but I still ask God to protect him from ungodly desires and give me the wisdom to handle them well, should they arise. The Bible says we are to obey God, above all.

We must obey God rather than men (Acts 5:29).

My fourth husband—the one I met, married, and divorced over a total of three months—kept trying to get me to go to a strip club for amateur night and was angry I refused. I wasn't a believer back then, but I still knew it was not appropriate, and I wasn't going to budge. He said I was being "unsubmissive."

Godly submission doesn't mean doing whatever your husband tells you to do. It means giving him opportunities to lead in ways that help him become a godly leader. If you submit to him in sin, you're helping him become an *ungodly* leader and allowing fear of his anger to control you more than your desire to please God.

Fear of man will prove to be a snare, but whoever trusts in the LORD is kept safe (Proverbs 29:25).

It goes without saying, but I'll say it anyway: if your husband is abusing you physically, remove yourself from the situation. Pray for God's protection, take appropriate legal measures to keep him from harming you or the children, and get biblical counseling. You can still respect and pray for him—from a safe distance.

C3 80

The family finances provide a great forum for practicing Active Submission. Whoever controls the checkbook makes most of the major decisions and approves or vetoes many of the others; so that person is, by default, often the leader of the family. Given that, and knowing it is through leadership God works most on your husband, it makes sense to create opportunities for him to lead in this area.

I used to have a saying, "You can mess with my heart, but don't mess with my credit," so I understand caution and reluctance to give up even an inch of financial control. In past marriages, I've had both separate accounts and joint accounts, but I've always managed "the money"—that is, anything having to do with paying bills or protecting our credit.

My current husband is responsible, generous, and easy-going, plus he's a former government auditor! Clearly, it was my own fears that kept me from trusting him to handle our finances. Add a dash of overconfidence in my own intelligence, the need to be in control, and typical concerns about financial solvency, and you get the idea. I took over, and patted myself on the back for doing so much for the family.

At first, he thought it was great not to have to worry about bills, budgets, and bank accounts; but before long, he began to feel as though he had no purpose in our marriage except to earn a paycheck and do whatever I said. That, in turn, directly and negatively impacted his desire to love and care for me. It's very hard for a man to love his wife when he doesn't feel good about himself.

It was several years before I was willing to give up dominion over our finances, and even then, I constantly looked over his shoulder and told him what to do. When I finally let go and decided to trust him, it was such a load off my back, I wondered why I had waited so long.

I'm fully aware you might have taken over the finances, not because you wanted to, but because you didn't have a choice. Some people are downright irresponsible with money, and giving a man like that control of the finances could be disastrous. You can, however, still look for ways to give him low-risk, low-emotion opportunities to practice and develop those financial and decision-making skills, safely.

First, you can ask him to pray for you to make wise decisions in whatever areas you manage. Over 90% of Americans say they pray, so it's a reasonable request—even if he's not a churchgoer or prayer is not a topic the two of you discuss. I've never known a man to be offended when his wife asked him to pray for her, especially when it was prefaced with the statement, "God says you're the leader of our family."

God says you are the leader of our family, so would you pray for me to make wise decisions when I'm working on the finances?

Those words may feel awkward to you, but they're powerful because they are God's truth. Don't tell him he *should be* the leader. God says he *already is,* and even an unbelieving man will eventually become curious about a God who says that.

Second, you can create Moments of Leadership by looking for low-risk decisions you can ask him to make, such as: how many days in advance of due-dates the bills should be paid, which of two amounts should be put into savings, how large of a payment should be made on a debt, or when to schedule a major household expenditure. By structuring the decision questions carefully, you can offer him leadership in such a way that any answer is financially acceptable. He gets to lead, you get to follow, and there's little danger of hurting the family's credit. As he grows in responsibility, you can give him leadership in more critical decisions.

It's a bit like "raising a husband," which may sound offensive; but the truth is, you've been trying to do that all along anyway—just wrongly. You've been acting as his teacher-mother instead of his helper-follower, giving him opportunities to obey and prove himself a "good boy," rather than opportunities to lead and prove himself a godly man.

What does all this look like, practically speaking? Instead of telling your husband about a decision you've made and expect him to abide by, turn that decision into a question and then honor his answer. You control the topic and the options, so it's safe, but he still gets to lead.

For example, instead of announcing, *"We need to buy a new stove,"* ask him, *"When would be a good time to buy a new stove?"* or, *"Would it be better to get a new stove this month or next?"* He may tell you he doesn't care *what* you do about the stove, and that's fine. Whether or not he steps into the opportunities you provide is up to God. Your responsibility is simply to offer them.

One young woman I know has a husband serving overseas in the military. She pays all of the bills, not only because he's away, but also because—by his own admission— he's "not good at that stuff." It's a lot of work, and she hopes he will become more involved when he comes home. Meanwhile, she's found a creative, no-risk way to start involving him now in their finances, and give him an opportunity for leadership.

In the past, whenever they had money left over at the end of the month, she would donate it to a charity of her choice—without asking his opinion. Now, she sends him an e-mail that recaps the monthly income and expenses, and asks what he thinks they should do with whatever is left over. She might offer some suggestions, but she honors his recommendations. I suspect receiving a note from his wife thousands of miles away, asking for his guidance as the leader of their home, means more to him than an entire boxful of "I love you" letters.

Another woman decided she and her husband needed to start setting aside some money each month. The conversation would normally have started with her telling him what they needed to do and criticizing him when he didn't agree:

She: "We need to start saving."

He: "We can't afford it."

She: "Well, you got that raise last month and we could put that away."

He: "We've got to pay off the credit card loan, plus there's some new gear I really need."

She: "You can't keep buying that stuff. We have to think about the future."

He: "I don't want to talk about it, right now."

She: "You always say that. You're so irresponsible!"

With a little coaching and role-playing in her small group beforehand, she approached it as an opportunity to give him a Moment of Leadership, instead:

She: *"God says you are the leader of our home,* so
     I'd like your thoughts on something."
He: "What?"
She: "I'm uncomfortable we aren't putting anything
     away in savings."
He: "We can't really afford it."
She: "I know what you mean, but can we take a look
     at our financial plans and budgets?"
He: "I guess so. Let's do that next Saturday."
She: "Okay. I'll be praying for wisdom when we
     look it over."
He: "Okay."

Her husband might still want to pay off their debt before saving—and there's biblical support for that approach—but he also might agree that saving is a good idea. The most unbiblical solution would be for his wife to insist on one thing or the other, taking the decision-making role away from him. Instead, she must pray and believe God *can* and *will* work through her husband for their benefit.

Lord, Show my husband how You would have us live in every area, particularly with regard to our finances. Help us put off ungodly financial habits and put on godly ones. Replace any anxiety or doubt we have with confidence in Your provision, and remind us to be generous in sharing that provision with others in need. Help us to be wise in how we spend our resources. Bless the work of our hands. In Jesus' Name. Amen.

⅌ ℞

Tithing is a particularly sensitive subject for many couples. In the following example, the wife is pretending to exercise Active Submission, but she's really just attempting to get her husband to do what she has already decided is best.

> She: "I read in the Bible that we need to be giving 10% to the church. I think we should."
> He: "Maybe. I don't know."
> She: "The Bible says so. You're the leader of the family and we need to do what the Bible says."
> He: "I know. I guess we should."
> She: "Look, here's the thing. I've already figured out that if we cut back on going out to eat, we can save about $100 and if you carpool we can save another $50. If I get my nails done at the other salon, that's $10. But that's still not 10% and we need to give 10%."
> He: "Ten percent will be too hard to do. We've got that credit card debt to pay off and the car loan. We should take care of that first."
> She: "If you didn't have to stop and get coffee every morning on your way to work we could tithe something. We have to obey God."

Now, look how the same conversation could have gone, had the wife been focused on true Active Submission and expressed her feelings without leading.

She: "I read in the Bible that we need to be giving
10% of our income to the church. I think we
should. *What do you think?"*

He: "Maybe. I don't know how we can."

She: *"God says you're the leader of our family,* so
I'll support whatever you think is best, but will
you pray about it before we talk more about it?"

He: "Sure."

She: "Thanks. Would it help if I pulled together our
bank statements for this year?"

He: "Yeah, that would be great."

She: "OK. With all the financial obligations we have
now, this will require some wisdom. I'll be
praying for you as the leader of our family, too.
I know it's not easy. I love you."

He: "Thanks. I love you, too."

Submission can be confusing at times. The Bible says to
tithe *and* to submit to a husband, but what if that husband
doesn't want to tithe? We either believe God knows what is
best for us and act on that, or we don't. If we tithe, volunteer at
the church, serve the poor, sing in the choir, and teach Sunday
School, but disobey God in the one commandment He gave
only to wives, I wonder how pleased He will be with us?

*Wives, submit to your husbands as to the Lord
(Ephesians 5:22).*

The fact is that godly outward behavior will never
compensate for a disobedient and untrusting heart. The solution

is to ask for wisdom and believe it will be given, according to James 1:5, "If any of you lacks wisdom, he should ask God, who gives generously to all, without finding fault, and it will be given to him," and Matthew 7:8, "For everyone who asks receives."

> *Lord, I know You tell us to tithe, but You also tell me to submit to my husband and he doesn't want to tithe. I am asking You, according to Your promises in Matthew 7:8 and James 1:5, to provide me with godly wisdom, generously and freely given, so that I might handle this situation in a way that will be pleasing to You. Give my husband wisdom, as well, and guide him in Your ways. Amen.*

03 80

Another area in which you can give your husband opportunities to grow in leadership is in his role as a father. I doubt he is a perfect parent, and I'm sure you disagree with some of his child-raising philosophies. He may be too lax or too strict, too soft or too harsh, but that doesn't affect your ability to give him Moments of Leadership. In fact, the *less* godly he is, the *more important* it is to do so. Let's follow a hypothetical situation as one mother turns a relatively minor, but common, school incident into such an opportunity.

Child: "Mom, my math teacher is really mean to me. He says I talk too much."
Mom: "Maybe you do talk too much."
Child: "No, I don't. My teacher just picks on me."

Normally, Mom might dismiss the complaint or find a way to resolve it on her own. If her husband is already leading the family, either of these would be a perfectly appropriate response. However, if he isn't, she can turn the situation into a Moment of Leadership by confirming Dad as the head of the family and inviting him to lead.

> Mom: "Hmm. Sounds like a tough problem. *God says Dad is the leader of our family.* Let's see what he says."
>
> Mom: (to Dad) *"God says you are the head of the family* and *we need your advic*e. Daughter thinks one of her teachers is picking on her."
>
> Child: (protesting to Dad) "I'm really good in that class. He just doesn't like me."

Dad's response may vary, depending on his level of spiritual maturity and wisdom. Here, we'll assume a godly response, one in which he also includes a biblical truth.

> Dad: (To Child) "My boss doesn't always like me, but I still have to obey him. *God tells us we have to submit to those who have authority over us.* Can you handle that?"
>
> Child: "I guess so."
>
> Dad: "Good. It won't be easy, but it's the right thing to do. When you're tempted to do the wrong thing, remember that. If you're still having problems next week, let's talk about it again."

Mom: *(creating another Moment of Leadership)*
"Would you pray for our daughter and for the teacher?"

Dad: "Sure."

If Dad is comfortable leading in prayer, he might do so right then. Otherwise, he might prefer to wait and pray for his daughter, privately. Either way, the child's conscience is pricked by the idea of her Dad's spiritual authority protecting and watching over her.

However, what if Dad had responded in an ungodly way?

Dad: "You probably *were* talking in class"

Child: "No, I wasn't."

Dad: "Don't talk back to me, young lady. You'd better start behaving at school."

Child: *(Rolls her eyes)*

Mom: *(Frustrated)* "You could at least give her some godly advice. You're her father."

Dad: *(Irritated)* "Stop pressuring me to be 'godly.' If you want her to have godly advice, then *you* give it to her."

Mom: *(To Child)* "Come on, let's go." *(Thinking, "Giving him a leadership opportunity sure didn't work. I won't do that again.")*

In that example, Mom made it clear she was disappointed in her husband, and she implied an "us against him" attitude by calling her daughter away with her. She modeled a "victim" role, which affirmed the child's similar reaction to her teacher.

What Mom needed to do was keep redirecting Dad toward Truth, without letting his ungodly attitude or imperfect authority distract her. She can do that no matter how he responds, modeling respectful submission to authority for her child, even when that authority is less than perfect. Her motivation must not be to make her husband "be godly," but to please God and trust in Him by standing on His Word.

> *Speaking the truth in love, we will in all things grow up into him who is the Head, that is, Christ (Ephesians 4:15).*

In the reframed dialogue below, notice how Mom's focus on Active Submission and Moments of Leadership helps her stay in control—and keeps her husband's ungodly responses from throwing her off track. She speaks the truth in love, and her peaceful confidence is clear, even in just the reading.

Dad: "You probably *were* talking in class"

Child: "No, I wasn't."

Dad: "Don't talk back to me, young lady. You'd better start behaving in class."

Child: *(Rolls her eyes)*

Mom: *(To Dad, overlooking the sin, affirming his position of spiritual headship, and redirecting his focus to God)* "The next time you pray, would you ask God to give our daughter wisdom in how He wants her to behave, and help her overcome any temptation to do otherwise?"

Dad:	(*Irritated*) "She knows how she should behave."
Mom:	"True, but since you're the leader of the family, your prayers would be helpful."
Dad:	"Ok, whatever."
Mom:	"Thanks."

Her husband didn't step into the leadership opening she provided, but she still spoke God's truth into his life, and God's Word does not return void.

> *It will . . . accomplish what I desire and achieve*
> *the purpose for which I sent it (Isaiah 55:11).*

CB ℬ

Your dominance may be a well-intentioned effort to take care of your family, but you are denying yourself—and your children—the joy and confidence of living under your husband's spiritual covering. Your prayers certainly provide protection for them, but even if you are "more spiritual" than your husband, you do not have the authority from God to be the family's spiritual leader and protector. Your husband does.

Few men start out godly, so don't despair if your marriage is far from where it should be and don't wait until your husband is more godly to begin Active Submission. I have seen, time and again, where a husband has unwittingly become an instrument of God's blessings for his wife, even when he thought he was only looking out for himself.

The king's heart is in the hand of the LORD; he directs it like a watercourse wherever he pleases (Proverbs 21:1).

A wife who isn't using her spiritual eyesight might miss how God answers her prayers through her husband, noticing only his self-centered motivation or his grumbling. But a wise woman will see through that noise and outward negativity, to what God is *really* doing through him.

Ah, Sovereign LORD, you have made the heavens and the earth by your great power and outstretched arm. Nothing is too hard for you (Jeremiah 32:17).

ප ශ්ප ශ

Chapter 7 - Suggested Prayers

Prayer for You

Heavenly Father,

I praise you, God. Thank you for giving me a husband who has different thoughts and ideas than I have. Teach me to listen to him with an open mind, and keep me from slipping into the sin of thinking my opinions are always best. Don't let my desires for efficiency or effectiveness give me a hard and unyielding heart.

Remind me that Active Submission isn't about trying to change my husband into the man I want him to be, but about trusting You to mold him into the man *You* want him to be. Show me where I can create Moments of Leadership for him, and help me see beyond outward appearances to the surprising and unexpected ways You are already moving in him. Give him ears to hear Your voice and the wisdom to listen to Your Words. In the Name of Jesus. Amen.

Prayer to Give to Your Husband

Heavenly Father,

I remember how close I felt to my wife when we were dating. I'd like to have that back again, and grow in our love for one another. Help me be a good and wise husband. May I never ask ungodly things of her or demand more than she is willing to give. In the Name of Jesus. Amen.

Chapter 7 - Homework

1. For two days, note what areas of your marriage your husband tends to make suggestions in and how you respond.

2. For five days, agree to your husband's suggestions in at least one of those areas, as an experiment. What differences do you notice in you or him? Share with a friend.

3. Practicing submission in order to please God means leaving the results up to God. Give a practical example from your life of how that is different than practicing submission in order to please your husband?

4. Memorize Hebrews 4:13. Use it in normal conversation in a way that gives hope. Write about how you used it.

5. Every relationship is unique when it comes to creating Moments of Leadership for a husband. Share a difficult experience with a friend, and role play to become comfortable turning it into a Moment of Leadership.

6. If you have children, do the same with ideas for situations involving them.

8. Chin Wagging

ecently, I saw a man walking with his wife in our neighborhood wearing a t-shirt that said, *"If a man speaks in the forest and there isn't a woman there to hear him, is he still wrong?"* I'll admit it made me laugh, but it also made me sad because it said a lot about the relationship between men and women. On his wife, that shirt would have seemed self-righteous and smug—a feminist commentary on the superiority of women and the foolishness of men. But he was the one wearing it.

Humor is the safest way to comment about a situation we are uncomfortable addressing directly, and wife dominance is such a prevalent trait in our culture that jokes and humorous references about it are not hard to find. Once I counted seven of them—on a Sunday morning.

Most were some variation of, *"Everyone knows a good husband is one who has learned to obey his wife,"* and all were accompanied by hearty laughter from the men. In fact, it was the men who usually *made* the comments. The wives just smiled and nodded at each other as if to say, *"Can you imagine what a mess they'd make of things without us?"*

⋘ ⋙

The Bible calls bossiness, "quarrelsomeness," and it must have been quite a problem back in King Solomon's day. He specifically warns men about it five times in the book of Proverbs.

> *A quarrelsome wife is like a constant dripping (Proverbs 19:1b).*

> *Better to live on a corner of the roof than share a house with a quarrelsome wife (Proverbs 21:9 and Proverbs 25:24).*

> *Better to live in a desert than with a quarrelsome and ill-tempered wife (Proverbs 21:19).*

> *A quarrelsome wife is like a constant dripping on a rainy day; restraining her is like restraining the wind or grasping oil with the hand (Proverbs 27:15-16).*

Most of us *are* quarrelsome—we just don't realize it. In an effort to keep our husbands from becoming the dominating beasts we were certain they could become, many of us became dominating beasts, ourselves. Don't ask our husbands. They'll just smile and say everything's fine. Ask them about some *other* man's wife, instead.

As one woman observed, "When I really listened to what I was saying, I discovered I 'shut my husband up' one way or another every time he opened his mouth. I thought I was just helping him make better decisions, but what I was doing was telling him he didn't know anything."

8. Chin Wagging

Here's a test: if you think you're "just being helpful" when you tell your husband what do, but bristle when he tells *you* what to do, you are quarrelsome. If you frequently tell him what he *should* do, what he *shouldn't* do, how he could do *better* what he's already doing, or how *wrong* he did something he's already done . . . you're quarrelsome.

Quarrelsomeness isn't always as obvious as you may think. See if you recognize yourself in these examples:

He: "Looks like it's going to rain today."
She: "No, I don't think so. "

He: "I like the chunky peanut butter."
She: "It's not as good. Get the creamy kind."

He: "Let's take the baby to the park."
She: "No, it's too hot and she needs her nap. "

He: "I'm going to go get the car cleaned."
She: "You better wait until tomorrow. It might rain. "

He: "Don't forget, my sister is coming today."
She: "I wish you hadn't invited her. She drives me crazy.

He: "The trash came early today."
She: "You should have put it out last night. "

He: "What a rough day. I'm exhausted."
She: "Don't leave your clothes on the floor. "

Treating a husband like a child is another form of bossiness or quarrelsomeness:

"Park over there."
"Drive slowly, now—this road is dangerous."
"Be careful, sweetheart."
"Don't forget your airplane ticket, darling."
"You'll need to take a sweater; it's cold outside."

Your husband may say he *likes* being reminded and being told what to do, but that's not the point. The point is, you have a holy responsibility to help your husband move into the fulfillment of what God has called him to be, and that means helping him be the leader of the family. If you short-circuit that process by treating him like a child, you will, in the long run, damage the marriage. Quarrelsomeness is so poisonous to a marriage and a husband's relationship with God that stopping it often results in immediate positive changes.

There are seven different types of quarrelsomeness, or what I call the "Seven Deadly C's." They are: complaining, condemning, conjecturing, contradicting, controlling, correcting, and criticizing. It's not important to remember each one, only that there are many ways words are used to establish dominance. They're "just words," but words can destroy.

If anyone considers herself religious and yet does not keep a tight rein on her tongue, she deceives herself and her religion is worthless (from James 1:26).

Have you ever *complained* about the way your husband loaded the dishwasher when he didn't do it the way you wanted? Don't be disappointed when he no longer helps clean in the kitchen. Complaining comes from pride and impatience.

> *No woman can tame the tongue. It is a restless evil, full of deadly poison (from James 3:8).*

How often do you *condemn* your husband? Condemnation is a form of self-righteousness that pushes him away. Here's the testimony of one young woman who caught herself condemning her husband, and how she turned it around.

> *I'd been feeling self-conscience about my weight lately and whenever I get that way, I always impose it on my husband, too. I guess whatever I am unhappy about with myself, I find the same fault in him. Anyway, I called him at work and heard a lot of noise:*

Me:	*"Where are you?"*
Him:	*"At the Mexican restaurant for lunch."*
Me:	*(Sarcastically) "Well that sounds just great."*
Him:	*"Well, I was excited about it. What are you doing?"*
Me:	*"Sitting here with the baby, deciding what to have for lunch. I was worried about eating healthy, but since you don't care that you're getting fat, I won't care about myself, either."*

Pretty horrible, huh? I thought about what you said about looking for sin in my own heart. I guess I can be pretty mean. A few hours later I called him back and could tell from his tone he was mad."

Me: *"What's wrong?"*
Him: *"Nothing."*
Me: *"You sound mad."*
Him: *"It just bugs me that every time I go out to eat, you judge me."*
Me: *"You're right, I'm sorry. I shouldn't impose my insecurities on you."*
Him: *(SILENCE)*
Me: *"Hello?"*
Him: *"Wow. That means a lot. Thank you!"*

I would have NEVER apologized before. I would have said something like, "Well, if you made better decisions, I wouldn't have to try to make you feel guilty." I'm so glad you taught me the importance of watching how my own sins can cause me to speak in ways that hurt him.

Do you *conjecture* or gossip? Do you say negative things about your husband's family? When he talks about other people, do you ask for all the details and then analyze their personalities and motivations? Maybe that's why he doesn't like to tell you what's going on. Gossip is a sin that destroys.

A gossip separates close friends (Proverbs 16:28).

8. Chin Wagging

Do you *contradict* your husband? That's why he's quit talking to you. Contradicting reveals the sins of pride and self-righteousness—and a lack of grace.

> *Out of the overflow of the heart the mouth speaks (Luke 6:45b).*

Do you try to *control* the way your husband behaves at home? That's why he withdraws and becomes less affectionate. The need to control is tied to a fear that your joy and contentment are in jeopardy. When you put your trust in God, there is no need to fear anything.

> *Surely God is my salvation; I will trust and not be afraid (Isaiah 12:2a).*

Do you *correct* your husband? Correction comes from the sins of pride and fear of criticism from others.

> *When my husband tells stories, it drives me crazy the way he makes up details he doesn't remember. I used to be all over him like a laser beam, zapping his inaccuracies. Boom! "No, it wasn't 2:30 on Wednesday in my car. It was Thursday at 8:00 in yours." "No, (dummy) it wasn't your brother who gave that to you, it was my Dad."*

> *If he said something that reflected poorly on me, I'd try to defend myself, and we'd end up tensely discussing who was right or wrong. I usually won the*

battle, but lost my pride. His listeners not only remembered what he had said—which normally they wouldn't—they also suspected I was guilty. Most of all, they wondered if I was always so quarrelsome.

Now, I try not to say anything to call attention to his mistakes and when it is something critical of me, I just smile as though he had paid me a compliment. It confuses his listeners, and the comment loses its impact. If what he said was really hurtful, I'll say something to him about it privately, later. Otherwise, I try to forgive him for being human, and drop it.

Do you *criticize* or negatively compare him to other men? He might act like it doesn't bother him, but being respected is one of the things a man values most, especially from his wife. Criticism comes from the sin of pridefulness.

Reckless words pierce like a sword, but the tongue of the wise brings healing (Proverbs 12:18).

You are the most important person in your husband's life, and when you speak disrespectfully to him, your words cut and worm their way into his heart. They bury themselves there, slowly eroding his ability to cherish you as you really want. Even when you're joking, it's risky business.

The wise woman builds her house, but with her own hands the foolish one tears hers down (Prv. 14:1).

You know that's true because the way he speaks to you influences how you feel towards him. My mother used to say, "If you can't say something nice, it's better to say nothing at all." The Bible puts it this way:

> *Do not let any unwholesome talk come out of your mouths, but only what is helpful for building others up according to their needs, that it may benefit those who listen (Ephesians 4:29).*

Men and women are different in this area. What builds your husband up is knowing he's respected; what builds you up is knowing you are loved. Unless he feels respected, being told how much you love him means little; and unless you feel loved, being told how much he respects you isn't going to make you want to jump into his arms.

Actions are just as important as words. The more you *demonstrate* respect through Active Submission, the more blessed your husband will feel to be married to you. The more blessed he feels, the more lovingly he will treat you.

> *Dear children, let us not love with words or tongue but with actions and in truth (1 John 3:18).*

You can't fake respect. If you think your husband is too far down to look up to, you've put yourself too high up in your own mind. Humble yourself and train your eyes to see him as a glorious creation of God, stained by sin, just as you are.

CB ⁊

Being dominating, bossy, or disrespectful to your husband can also cause problems with your children. As mentioned in the last chapter, if you assume the leadership position, you put your children and yourself outside the will of God—which leads to temptation and sin.

Additionally, when they see from your example that their father is not worthy of respect, they become disobedient to him and other authority, including God—and you. As they get older, they'll be suspicious that when they are ready to begin taking control of their own lives as adults, you will frustrate them by dominating them the way you dominate your husband.

> *My brothers, can a fig tree bear olives, or a grapevine bear figs? Neither can a salt spring produce fresh water (James 3:12).*

Cß ßO

Now, let's see how a wife who's started practicing Active Submission would have responded to her husband in the quarrelsomeness examples given at the beginning of this chapter. These may seem patronizing when you read them, but they're not.

He: "Look's like it's going to rain today."
She: *"Maybe so."*

He: "I like the chunky peanut butter better than smooth."
She: *"Okay. How about getting one of each?"*

8. Chin Wagging

He: "Let's take the baby to the park."

She: *"Sounds great. How about 2:00 so she can get her nap and be in a good mood?"*

He: "I'm going to go get the car cleaned."

She: *"That's thoughtful. Thanks for taking good care of us."*

He: "Don't forget, my sister is coming to visit Sunday."

She: *"I know. It's hard for me when she visits, will you pray for me to be patient and kind?"*

He: "The trash came early today."

She: *"Wow. It sure did."*

He: "What a rough day."

She: *"Really?"*

I'm not saying wives are the cause of everything wrong in a marriage, but I *am* saying you have far more influence than you realize. The words you say and the things you do have a direct impact on how your husband feels and acts—even more than the impact his words and behaviors have on you. That's hard to believe, I know, and I don't expect you to agree until you see it for yourself, but you won't see it unless you try.

You've been begging God to touch your husband's heart, yet He's given *you* the ability to make possible the very thing you've been asking Him to do. Your husband won't really change until he's leading, and he can't lead unless you choose to follow him. The first step has to begin with you.

Wives, in the same way be submissive to your husbands so that, if any of them do not believe the word, they may be won over without words by the behavior of their wives, when they see the purity and reverence of your lives (1 Peter 3:1-2).

How ironic it is that the one area we have *rejected* the most—submission—holds the spiritual key to unleashing God's power in the one area of change we have *longed* for the most: a husband's heart. It's been right in front of us the whole time.

Those verses from 1 Peter say that submission can convince a man to believe in Christ. If it can do that to an unbelieving heart, imagine what it can do to a believing one.

3 80C3 80

Chapter 8 ~ Suggested Prayers

Prayer for You

Father,

I confess I have been quarrelsome and I repent. Change my heart to one that respects my husband as the man *You* want Him to be, instead of the man he is or the man *I* want him to be. Remind me that *"faith is being sure of what I hope for and certain of what I cannot see" (Hebrews 11:1)*. Make the words of my mouth kind and wise. Help me encourage him instead of tearing him down. Help me appreciate his strengths and efforts, instead of criticizing his weaknesses and failures.

Forgive me for judging my husband in ways I wouldn't let anyone judge me, and for treating him in ways I would not want to be treated. You didn't make me his wife in order to make him more perfect, but to perfect me. Show me what idols I have hidden in my heart and help me overcome them through the power of the Holy Spirit. In Jesus' Name. Amen.

Prayer to Give to Your Husband

Father,

Show us how our words tear down love and build up walls between us. Give us wisdom to see our own sins and overcome them so that we can be the way You would have us be. In Jesus' Name. Amen.

Chapter 8 – Homework

1. Keep a log for several days before trying to eliminate the Seven Deadly C's. How many are you guilty of? Which one(s) do you do most often? Give the details of a few situations. What sins or idols were at the root of your behavior? Share with a friend and discuss.

2. See how long you can go without being guilty of one of the Seven Deadly C's. Document your progress. Note some situations when it was really difficult. Share with a friend.

3. Memorize Proverbs 14:1. Find three opportunities to speak it into your friends' lives in a relevant, practical, and loving way. Write down their names and the dates.

9. Joy of Obedience

By the time Valentine's Day arrived, I had been practicing Active Submission and Moments of Leadership for about six weeks, primarily by agreeing to my husbands suggestions and not being quarrelsome. There was still some tension between us, but things were definitely improving. We were *both* starting to grow.

That evening, I rushed home from an eleven-hour workday to change clothes for the church's Sweetheart Banquet across town. My husband, who was between assignments at the time, had been relaxing all day and was already dressed. As soon as I was ready, we hurried out the door, climbed into the car and buckled our seatbelts, when he turned to me and asked, "Did you get the directions?"

There was dead silence. Normally, I would have thought to myself, *"He could have done that himself, but I want to please him, and I don't want to ruin the evening. I can get them faster and better than he can, anyway."* Then I would have jumped out of the car, run in the house in my heels, looked up the address on the computer, and printed out a map.

While waiting for the printer, my thoughts would have shifted to: *"Why is it my job? I'm doing everything else. Why doesn't he take some responsibility instead of always expecting me to do everything? He had all day to get the map. It's not fair. I'm working too hard, and he's hardly working."*

I would have come out with the directions, but it wouldn't have had anything to do with submission, being loving, or being his helper. How could it have? I thought *I* was the one who needed a helper, not him.

By the time we arrived at the banquet, I would have been steaming: *"How dare he expect me to get directions when I've been working all day. He is so self-centered and lazy. I'm tired of this!"* I wouldn't have said anything, but you can bet I would have made sure he knew by my body language that I was not at all pleased. Dinner would have been strained, at best.

Instead, when we got in the car, I was so focused on pleasing God that when he asked if I had the directions, I just looked at him and said with calm respect, "No, sweetheart. You are the leader of our family, and I trust you to take care of us."

I'm not sure who was more surprised—him or me. Those were not words I would normally have used. The Holy Spirit must have been moving in us, because my husband turned back to me with the strangest look on his face and said, "Oh, okay." Then he went into the house to print the map.

Some people might have said being submissive would have meant getting the directions—and in some cases it would have, especially if he had specifically asked me to get them. That night, however, we experienced the husband-leadership dynamic more powerfully by me exhibiting confidence he would take care of us and solve the problem.

I have a confession to make, though. Once we were on our way, I had to fight the urge to give him advice on how he could have made a better map. I couldn't believe the thought even crossed my mind, given what had just happened, and it made me aware of how diligently I needed to guard against old habits.

Dinner that night ended up being one of the most incredible evenings we have ever had. Talk about God working miracles and changes! The transformation in my husband was amazing. He was attentive, adoring, and affectionate—and every bit as romantic as if he had just fallen in love with me for the very first time.

Delight yourself in the LORD and he will give you the desires of your heart (Psalm 37:4).

છ ૪૭

Things didn't always go as well as they did that night, though. One morning, a couple of weeks later, we were coming in from a walk when he asked if I would like to play a round of golf that afternoon.

"Sure," I said, still practicing Moments of Leadership.

"Okay, get us a tee time while I get my shower," he said.

When I golf by myself—or with other women—I don't mind dealing with the pro shop, but it feels uncomfortable when he and I are playing as a couple. There's also the inconvenient fact that being told what to do puts me in a "fight or flight" mode. Remembering how well Valentine's Day had gone, I tried the same line again.

"Honey, you're the leader of our family, and I'd feel more comfortable if you made the tee-time."

The only problem was, this time it really *was* a line; and I was trying to change his behavior, instead of trying to please God. Also, he had specifically asked me to do something—and my resistance put us on a collision course.

"I don't know the number," he said. "*You* call them."

"No," I replied. "I feel funny about it. You can look it up."

"If you don't call, then we just won't go," he said.

Now, I could discuss *his* behavior, but Active Submission focuses on my own heart, not his. I prayed silently as we walked in the house:

> *Lord, I want to honor You, but where do I go from here? Don't let me be petty. Show me how I can react in a way that is pleasing to You.*

I didn't consciously decide what to do next. I just walked over to where we kept the phone books and looked up the clubhouse listing. Then I said, "I'll get the number and you can call them, okay?" He agreed, we had a great time, and that was that. My pride had kept me from submitting to his original request with a joyful heart, but when I refocused on pleasing God, He showed me a way out.

It was a great lesson, and I was thankful to learn it.

> *No temptation has seized you except what is common to man. And God is faithful; he will not let you be tempted beyond what you can bear. But when you are tempted, he will also provide a way out so that you can stand up under it (1 Corinthians 10:13).*

I have another confession: I had to bite my tongue not to interrupt him and suggest a "better" tee-time while he was on the phone. No wonder he always told me to call. I thought he hadn't wanted to be our leader because he was uncomfortable in the role. Now, I realized I might have just nagged him out of it.

Not only had God turned around a situation I had effectively "blown," He had used it to reveal sin in my heart that wouldn't have been revealed if I had handled it correctly to begin with. He really *was* able to work all things for good when I was intent on pleasing Him.

> *And we know that in all things God works for the good of those who love him, who have been called according to his purpose (Romans 8:28).*

A few days later, my husband went out of town and left a note on the kitchen table, addressed to me.

> *Sweetheart, I love you and will miss you. Here are some scripture verses I thought we could study and pray about together while I'm gone. They seem to apply to our lives right now.*

I don't even remember now what the verses were, although I wish I did. What touched me so deeply was that he had first, left me such a sweet note; and second, he had suggested we study the Bible together. Never, in all the years we had been married had he done that. It was a two-hanky read; but through my tears, I was smiling.

What God had shown me was true. My obedience to step aside and give my husband room to grow in his leadership was really making a difference in how we felt about each other. The more I gave him opportunities to lead, the more loving he became and the more I loved him. It reminded of God's challenge in the book of Malachi.

> *"Test me in this," says the LORD Almighty, "and see if I will not throw open the floodgates of heaven and pour out so much blessing that you will not have room enough for it" (Malachi 3:10).*

That verse is about tithing money, but I think it applies to our hearts and lives as well. As I learned to tithe joyful obedience, blessing after blessing started coming into our marriage.

> *Blessed . . . are those who hear the word of God and obey it (Luke 11:28).*

I had experienced the comfort of God through prayer and the glory of God through praise, but I had never been told about this incredible joy of obedience. It was like turning a key in the doors of the Kingdom of Heaven and standing in the presence of God.

ೞ ೫ೞ ೫

Chapter 9 ~ Suggested Prayers

Prayer for You

Lord,

Thank you for my husband. Sometimes I forget that submission isn't about obeying him, but about obeying You. Keep that truth fresh in my mind at all times so that resentment and wrong-thinking don't creep into my heart. Remind me to trust that You know what is best for me and You can work through my husband to show me and grow me. Give me the willingness to see myself from *his* eyes, the wisdom to see myself from *Your* eyes, and the grace to learn from my mistakes.

Bless my husband and the work of his hands. Soften his heart to recognize the changes in me as a sincere desire to please You. Fill us both with the desire to obey You simply because we love You and want to remain in Your love. In Jesus' Name I pray. Amen.

Prayer to Give to Your Husband

Lord,

You say You are my authority, and I am the head of the family. Remind me that obeying You is a joy. *"Your commands are not burdensome, for everyone who is born of God overcomes the world" (1 John 5:3-4).* Bless our marriage. In Jesus' name I pray. Amen.

Chapter 9 ~ Homework

1. One of the themes of the Old Testament is how quickly people forget God's powerful love and provision in their lives and slipped back into disobedience. Take time to jot down a few of blessings have seen in your marriage through your obedience. Give specific examples and stories so you can share them with other women. Become a living testimony of God's goodness.

2. Memorize Luke 11:28. Speak it into two people's lives this week. Write down their names and the dates.

3. Share three examples where you made a determined effort to obey the Lord by giving your husband a Moment of Leadership. Tell what happened.

SECTION THREE

Growing

10. The Blessing

For nearly a decade of marriage, I lived by the philosophy, "It's easier to beg forgiveness than ask permission."[12] If I wanted to do something, I made the commitment first and then told my husband about it afterwards.

Sometimes, I'd pretend to ask up front, but it was just a set-up to prevent him from getting mad at me later. I knew exactly what to say to get him to agree to whatever I wanted. Inevitably, when the reality of time and financial costs sank in, he would grow distant, and I would protest, "You agreed, and now you act like this. What am I supposed to do?" It may have seemed like harmless posturing to justify getting my way, but it was manipulative deceit—and deceit is a sin.

She who plots evil with deceit in her heart—she always stirs up dissension (from Proverbs 6:14).

I began to wonder how I could use Active Submission in this area. If you think about it, it makes sense. My husband is a smart man who knows and loves me better than anyone else. He is the only person who can anticipate what kind of impact my activities will have on him, and the only one—besides me— who can anticipate the consequences on our marriage.

It was foolish of me not to get his viewpoint and blessing on decisions that used our money or took away from our time together. It was also foolish to think God wouldn't use him to guide me. I'm heavily influenced by my wants and desires, and I'm not always inclined to listen to what God has to say.

The first opportunity I had to put the concept of "The Blessing" into action was with regard to a sixteen-week class on missions. Normally, I would have just signed up for the class and told my husband after the fact. He wouldn't have objected—at least not until the realities of my being gone every Wednesday had sunk in. Then, he would have been discontented and grumpy, and I would have had to pretend I didn't notice his negativity, while secretly resenting it.

This time, I got a copy of the textbook first and asked him to look through it. "I'd like to know if you think it would be a good investment of our time and money for me to take this class, and if you could bless my participation."

I suspected he would immediately say it was fine, but he didn't. He took my request seriously and spent several hours looking through the text. Strangely, it felt good he cared.

He concluded it would be a great idea, and not once did he seem resentful or hurt about the time I spent away. In fact, he attended class with me occasionally and even went in my place when I was out of town. Gone was the stress of guilt and self-righteousness I used to feel, and in its place was peaceful confidence. He had blessed my taking the class, and it had become something we shared, instead of a source of tension.

10. The Blessing

Many times after that incident, I looked for ways to ask for his blessing before doing something, and he always gave it—whether it was something small like a household purchase, or something large like a ministry visit to a third world country. The real test came when I asked about a trip I had hoped to take to the Middle East. After praying about it, he said, "I'd rather you not go at this time." Then he added, "But it's up to you."

I paused to consider the facts. There were safety and financial concerns, of course, but I had been privately hoping to take the trip for over a year. I knew if I insisted, he would easily give in. On the other hand, I had come to enjoy the protection of his blessing over my activities, and I was beginning to sense what having his spiritual covering meant. I realized I didn't want to go on such a dangerous trip without it.

No doubt, had I gone, there would have been wonderful pictures and stories to share, and he would have been happy for me. But under the surface, in the spiritual foundation of our marriage, tiny hairline fractures would have appeared.

Those fractures would have represented disregard for his guidance, lust for my own desires, and disobedience to God's command to honor my husband. They would have weakened the progress we had made in our marriage, and I would have lost some of the closeness to God—and to my husband—that obeying God had brought. Nothing was worth that.

I had also grown in my confidence that God worked *through* my husband on my behalf. Although I might never know the details, I trusted God had His reasons why I shouldn't go. I would never have heard that still small voice in the clamor of my own desires; but my husband had, and I chose to be grateful for his love and leadership, rather than resentful of his

123

reluctance for me to go. It was a watershed decision for both of us—evidence that submission wasn't just something I pretended to do because I knew I would get what I wanted.

I was encouraged. So far, in my experiment, I hadn't become a doormat, and my husband hadn't become a tyrant. In fact, if anything, he had become *more* loving, and I had become stronger and more confident in our relationship.

C3 &O

Recently, it was my husband who had a hard decision to make. It was tempting to ask him for the details so I could help calculate a solution and tell him what to do. Instead, I listened as he agonized over his options; and then, I encouraged him to go to God for wisdom, and to godly, believing, male friends for additional counsel.

Plans fail for lack of counsel, but with many advisers they succeed (Proverbs 15:22).

When he specifically asked what I thought he should do, I offered my analysis of the pros and cons—without drawing a conclusion—and resisted the temptation to come up with one in my own mind. Instead, I suggested we pray about it. He surprised me by having us kneel, right then, as he prayed aloud for wisdom. It was a special moment, one we would have missed it had I taken over and told him what to do.

Over the next few days, I let him know I was continuing to lift him up in prayer and assured him that whatever he decided, I would stand with him. The next week, it was like a dark cloud had lifted from his spirit. He shared his decision with me and the biblical principles he had relied upon to make that decision. Nothing I could have offered would have had nearly the impact on his faith as the time he spent seeking God's guidance, and nothing would have meant as much to me as seeing him draw nearer to the Lord.

Another time, he was in the midst of making a particularly life-changing career decision about which I had a tremendous sense of unease. Rather than try to change his mind, I shared my discomfort and told him I was praying that God would either give me peace about it if it was right, or reveal to him things he might have overlooked if it wasn't. I waited, resisting the temptation to bring it up again. Within a week, he had changed his mind—for the very same reasons that had concerned me—without my having said another word about it.

CB &O

I didn't even know how to pray for my husband until six years ago. We had been waiting for a plane and were in disagreement about something, so I had taken a walk through the terminal to get a break from the tension. As I passed a bookstore, *The Power of a Praying Wife*[13] caught my eye.

I picked it up and read through a few of the prayers, then purchased it and returned to the gate where my husband was waiting. By the time I got there, he was a different man—not at all the grouchy grump he had been when I left for my walk. I wasn't sure if it had been the prayers I had read, or just coincidence, but it was enough to make me want to continue praying for him.

Two years later, I bought him the companion book, *The Power of a Praying Husband*, hoping he would begin praying for me, as well. You can guess it sat around untouched—despite being left in a number of obvious places. After eighteen months of unsuccessful "hinting," I wrote in the front cover how much it would mean to know he was praying for me and slipped it into his carry-on bag as he headed out of town on business. Then, I waited nervously.

He made no mention of it while he was gone, but when he returned, he proudly showed me how every prayer had a handwritten date by it. He has continued to pray for me daily, and now, that book and his Bible are the first two things he puts in his carry-on bag when he travels. I've grown so accustomed to living under his spiritual covering that I can actually *sense* when he's fallen out of the habit.

Every now and then, with his permission, I'll look through that little book, running my finger down the long rows of handwritten dates and reading the short notes he's added here and there. Next to my own Bible, it has become one of my most treasured possessions—enduring evidence of my husband's love and protection over me.

 beta beta beta beta

Chapter 10 - Suggested Prayers

Prayer for You

Dear Lord,

Thank You for the many ways You bless me through my husband. Give him the discernment to make wise decisions for our family, especially regarding our time together and our finances. I trust You to speak to me, through him, about things I might not be willing to hear if You tried to tell me directly.

When he is troubled by a decision, quiet my inclination to try to solve his problems or impose my will on him, so He can seek Your will with a clear mind. Give me a heart that listens to his concerns with love and patience, instead of anxiety or fear. Remind me to pray daily for him, even as you bless his spiritual leadership over our home. In Jesus' Name. Amen.

Prayer to Give to Your Husband

Dear Lord,

Give me wisdom to make good decisions for our family, and remind me to turn to You when I am not sure what to do. Watch over my wife today and remind me to pray for her often. Help us love each other as you want us to. In Jesus' Name. Amen.

Chapter 10 ~ Homework

1. What was the most recent thing you did, that you didn't tell your husband about until later, because you thought he might disapprove? Describe your emotions before, during, and after.

2. Can you think of a time when you felt manipulated into going along with something you really didn't want to do?

3. Think of at least one decision or activity this week that you can ask your husband's blessing on before committing to it. Role-play with a friend before approaching your husband. Be sure to include godly language, such as, "God says you're the leader of our family . . ." Share what happened.

11. Alpha Behavior

A number of years ago, there was a television documentary on dog obedience, that showed how packs of dogs jostle with each other through intimidation and fighting to determine the leader or "Alpha" dog. The rest of the pack acknowledges the Alpha through *submissive* body language and posturing, and he maintains his authority by exercising *dominant* body language.

The reason the show stayed with me was because it said pet dogs also implement Alpha behavior with their owners. For example, if your dog rests with his paw or head on top of your foot or stares at you, he's in effect saying, "I'm the boss and you're not." I remember being disappointed that what I had thought were signs of affection from my dog were really just indications she thought she was my superior.

This all came to mind during church one Sunday as I casually and lovingly started to put my arm around my husband's shoulders. Suddenly, I jerked it back. *"Was I exhibiting Alpha behavior?"* I wondered, with a shock. *"Was I saying, 'I'm the boss,' with my body language?"*

It had been fun looking for ways I dominated in our marriage, but this one made me laugh. Yet, it was so obvious. I *always* dominated my husband with my body language. I threw my legs over his when we watched television together, I put my arm around him when we sat close, I wrapped my limbs around him when we slept. I even stared at him expectantly, trying to get his eye. *"Why won't he look at me?"* I thought. No wonder.

It was strange in a way, to consider that something as unrelated as Alpha dog behavior might play a role in Active Submission. *"Was I really feeling dominant when I did that?"* I didn't think so. I thought I was just lovingly reaching out and being affectionate—but I was game for anything, and it was worth a try.

So I stopped all Alpha behaviors. When we slept, I moved next to my husband, but kept my arms and legs to myself. When I touched him, I slipped my arm *under* his, instead of on top of it. There were even little things I did differently, like standing close and waiting for him to reach out to me, instead of reaching out to him.

Stopping those behaviors helped me recognize some emotions I hadn't realized I was having. Sometimes, I wanted to pull him close because I felt he was being emotionally distant. Other times, frankly, it was an attempt to make up for previous not-so-positive thoughts. The unspoken sentiment was something like, *"You know, I really do love you, after all, even though just yesterday I was thinking what a bum you are. You're not all that bad, really."* It was a private atonement.

Amazingly, the more I *quit* behaving like the strong protector/provider, the more he *started* doing so. He began putting his arm around me, holding me when we slept, and taking my hand. It was like a vacuum he instinctively filled—and the more affectionate he acted, the more affectionate he seemed *to feel.*

Soon, I was noticing Alpha behavior in other women, everywhere. At the movie theater, I watched a young woman nearly suffocate her date with it. She wrapped herself around him, played with his hair, and gave him little kisses. He just stood there in line, one arm loosely around her waist, looking embarrassed. She obviously craved his affection, but her efforts made him look more like a beloved child than a man, and he was closing down. How could he be strong and manly with her when she wasn't leaving him an opening to do so?

Recently, a man sitting a few rows in front of us at church put his arm around his wife. His loving gesture was what initially caught my eye, but it was her response that fascinated me. No sooner had his arm rested on her shoulder, than she responded by putting her arm *on top of his* and around *his* shoulders. She had just trumped his body language with hers—and she didn't even know it.

He quickly pulled his arm back and put it meekly in his lap. Then he lowered his head and slumped his shoulders. She raised her head a little higher, sat straighter, and lightly caressed his shoulder with her finger tips. Their body language couldn't have been clearer: she was the Alpha, the boss, the strong one of the family—the one who protected and cared for *him*.

It's a common mistake for strong women to give their husbands the kind of protective, nurturing love they desire for themselves. Unfortunately, to their husbands, that feels like mothering and causes them to pull away. Not understanding the power of Active Submission, their wives try harder to pull them closer, only to end up pushing them away or "one-upping" them, even when they *do* try to lead.

The woman in that pew not only lost an opportunity to let her husband be a godly leader and express his affection, she established *herself* as the head of the family. It was such a small thing, lasting only a second or two, but it was a powerful statement with relational consequences. I am certain, had I asked, she would have said she wished her husband took charge of things more often.

Alpha behavior is so obvious that it's usually the first thing I notice when my controlling, dominating ways start creeping in again. It's become kind of an early-warning alarm system. If I catch myself wanting to throw a leg over my husband at night, I think back over the day and can almost always identify ways I've started trying—or at least *thought* about trying—to control and change him. Strange, but true.

CB &

Another type of dominant behavior I engaged in was using body language to control our communication. For example, when my husband asked me a question, I would start walking away and toss an answer over my shoulder to him. He wouldn't hear it and he'd ask me again. Annoyed, I'd return part way, turn around, and do the same thing—sometimes more than once. My voice may have been calculatingly polite, but my behavior spoke louder than my words.

Haughty eyes and a proud heart, the lamp of the wicked, are sin (Proverbs 21:4).

Similarly, if he interrupted something I was doing to talk to me, I would smile; but my body language would say, *"What's the matter with you, can't you see how busy I am?"* Later on, I'd complain we didn't spend enough time together, just talking. I'm ashamed to admit this didn't happen once or twice, but all the time, and he knew it. I can't imagine how hurtful and disrespectful it felt to him. I wanted interaction with him all right—but only *when* I wanted it, to discuss *what* I wanted, on *my* terms.

> *The good woman brings good things out of the good stored up in her heart, and the evil woman brings evil things out of the evil stored up in her heart (from Luke 6:45).*

These sin areas, or moments of disrespect, were easy to turn into Moments of Leadership and respect, using Active Submission. I started giving him my undivided attention when he was talking and made a point to answer his questions directly, instead of over my shoulder. When he interrupted my work to tell me something, I stopped what I was doing and engaged in the conversation. Basically, I treated him the way I wanted to be treated.

> *Do to others as you would have them do to you (Luke 6:31).*

Another area of disrespect showed itself when we were getting ready to go somewhere. Inevitably, my husband would be ready before I was, and then he'd tell me it was "time to go."

I wasn't necessarily running late, but his announcement annoyed me. "Okay," I'd respond, instinctively slowing down to buck his control. I wasn't deliberately trying to be rude; it was just a knee-jerk reaction. Well, maybe it *was* deliberate—maybe I wanted him to get the message he wasn't going to tell me what to do.

It's pretty sad, if you think about it. I had criticized him for not being responsible; and there I was, resisting him in the very area where he was showing responsibility. *"What if he hadn't cared about being on time and always made us late?"* I could talk a good game about being willing to let him lead, but I still struggled with submission when it wasn't my choice.

Again, first I had to privately examine my heart, confess, and repent. Only then could I begin to see his actions as responsible and caring. Next, I began to show appreciation and respect for his care. I tried to be ready when he wanted to go, even asking him earlier in the day what time he would like to leave. If I ran late, I didn't give him a vague, "almost" answer, but an honest assessment of exactly how many more minutes I needed.

There were plenty of times I forgot my lipstick or, as we were walking out the door, realized my outfit didn't match as well as I had thought. It was tempting to make a fuss about it and ask him to wait while I fixed the problem, but I refrained. No one noticed, anyway. He certainly didn't. What he *did* notice was how I honored him by respecting his desire to be on time—and he walked beside his unlipsticked, mismatched wife as though she were the most beautiful woman on earth.

CB ᘔCB ᘔ

Chapter 11 - Suggested Prayers

Prayer for You

Dear God,

You are so amazing. Thank you for giving me life. Bless our marriage and continue to build us up in love for one another. Show me ways I can create openings for my husband to demonstrate his protection, provision, and care for our family. Give me confidence in his ability to do these things, even when he doesn't have confidence in himself. Let me be a quiet encourager, one who has faith in her husband.

Help me see him as Your awesome creation, designed in perfection, though he struggles with sin. Bless his strength and manliness; and show me how I can give him opportunities to demonstrate that strength in positive, godly ways. Make me mindful of my body language, knowing it conveys the things of the heart. Bring my actions in line with Your commands and my heart in line with Your Will. In Jesus' name. Amen.

Prayer to Give to Your Husband

Dear God,

You are so amazing. Thank you for giving me life. Thank you for my wife. Bless our marriage and help me be a good provider and protector. Keep showing each of us where we need to grow and change, especially in the ways we show affection to one another. In Jesus' name. Amen.

Chapter 11 ~ Homework

1. Can you think of any Alpha body language you engage in with your husband?

2. Stop doing those Alpha behaviors for one week. Note your observations.

3. Observe other women and note how often you see Alpha behaviors.

12. Mirroring

Women are like Windows® Operating Systems. We keep multiple programs open in our minds simultaneously, with financial and operational efficiency programs filtering everything in the background. We can switch back and forth as quickly as a mouse-click, in the blink of an eye.

Men, on the other hand, are like pre-Windows DOS. Not that they're old fashioned or slow, but they're linear thinkers with only one "program" open at a time. That's why they don't hear us when they're watching television, reading, eating, working—or doing anything else for that matter. Most of them don't process more than one stream of information at a time.

Nowhere is this more obvious than in conversation. It's one thing for us to have a rapid-fire give-and-take with our girlfriends—we can each hold our own. It's another thing for us to talk the same way to our husbands. I should say, *try* to talk to them that way.

Chances are, we'll talk, and they'll pretend to listen. Faced with what seems to be a whirlwind of words and thoughts coming from our mouths, they'll nod politely and retreat into single syllable responses. They simply don't have time to process it all.

CB ED

Two men having a conversation may *seem* to be talking as fast as two women, but listen closely and you'll realize the pace of their information exchange is much slower. They use broad brush descriptions, repeat what the other just said, and ask questions to which they expect an answer. Here are two good friends, Trey and Chris, discussing a game they watched the night before:

Trey: "The team played great last night. Did you see that last inning?"

Chris: "Yeah. Good inning. Johnson's homer was something."

Trey: "What a hit! Weak pitching in the third inning, though."

Chris: "Yeah, it was weak. I hope he gets his arm back before next game."

Trey: "Me, too. We need him. Next game should be good, though. You gonna' watch it?"

Chris: "Sure."

Women, on the other hand, springboard from topic to topic, weaving several subjects together. It's difficult for them to refrain from gossip, which not only adds additional information, it also lengthens the conversation. They use rhetorical questions to introduce new information or express emotion, and they often answer their own questions. Trey and Chris's wives, talking about the same game, might have sounded like this:

Kendra: "The team played great last night. Did you see that last inning? It was amazing."

Lauren: "Yeah. It was great. Gordon seemed a little off his game; do you think it had anything to do with the family problems that were in the news yesterday? They said his wife, Alyssa, was out of the country, and his mom had to take his little girl to the hospital."

Kendra: "Maybe. I wish they'd leave him alone. It can't be easy to play when your child is in the hospital like that. Did you read that the doctors think she probably broke her leg in two places? I had a neighbor who did that once and it was months before he was healed. Oh my gosh, you should have seen how mean he was while he had that cast on."

Lauren: "That's so sad . . . what do you think about starting a prayer chain? I think we should. You know, I broke my leg once, and the prayer chain meant a lot to me."

Kendra: "That's right, I remember. Let's do start a prayer chain. I'll call Susan. I need to talk to her about the banquet next month, anyway. Hey, I'm running to the grocery. Anything you need? I can pick it up for you.

A man would have had a difficult time following that conversation. In fact, he'd probably still be thinking about answering Kendra's first question, while she had already moved on to other topics. That's why, when Trey goes home and talks about the game with his wife, Lauren, their differing conversation styles collide:

Trey: "The team played great last night. Did you see that last inning?"

Lauren: "Yeah. It was great. Gordon seemed a little off his game; do you think it had anything to do with the family problems that were in the news yesterday? They said his wife was out of the country, and his mom had to take his little girl to the hospital."

Trey: "What?"

Lauren: "I *said*, Gordon's wife, Alyssa, was out of the country, and his mom had to take his little girl to the hospital. I wish they'd leave him alone. It can't be easy to play when your child is in the hospital like that. Did you read that the doctors think his daughter probably broke her leg in two places? I had a neighbor who did that once and it was months before he was healed. Oh my gosh, he was so mean while he had that cast on."

Trey: *(Having tuned her out)* "Uh huh."

Lauren: "Are you listening to me? I'm thinking I should start a prayer chain. What do you think? It meant a lot to me when I broke my leg."

Trey: "OK"

Lauren: "Hey, I'll call Susan. She can help. I need to talk to her about the banquet next month anyway . . . I'm going to the store. Is there anything you want? Trey! *Hello. Are you listening to me? You never listen!*"

Lauren included so many different subjects, so many rhetorical questions, and so many words, Trey wasn't able to follower her, so he stopped listening. If she wants him to hear her, she needs to slow down and mirror his style and pace of communication.

Trey: "The team played great last night. Did you see that last inning?"

Lauren: "Yeah. It was great. Gordon seemed a little off his game, though.

Trey: "Yeah. Weak pitching in the third inning.

Lauren: "It was weak. Hopefully he'll get with it next game."

Trey: "He needs to get his arm back. Next game should be good. Want to watch it?"

Lauren: "I'd enjoy seeing it." *(Pausing, to change topic)* As an aside, did you know about Gordon's daughter?"

Trey: "What?"

Lauren: "Gordon's daughter has a broken leg.

Trey: "I didn't know that."

Lauren: "It's true. Do you think it would be a good idea for me to ask the ladies to pray for her?"

Trey: "Sounds like a nice idea."

Lauren: *(Acknowledging she heard him)* "Thanks." *(Pause)* "Changing the subject . . ."

Trey: "Yes?"

Lauren: "I'm going to the grocery store in a little while. Anything you'd like me to pick up?"

Notice how Lauren repeated Trey's thoughts, answered his questions, and asked him *real* questions, without answering them herself. She stayed on each subject until it reached a conclusion and then let Trey know she was making a topic change. By mirroring his pace, she made it more comfortable for him to communicate and also—by the way—turned the conversation into a Moment of Leadership by following his pace.

The idea of mirroring isn't new. Paul teaches it to his disciples in his first letter to the Corinthians:

> *To the Jews I became like a Jew, to win the Jew; to those under the law, I became as one under the law (though I myself am not under the law), so as to win those under the law. . . . I have become all things to all men so that by all possible means I might save some (from 1 Corinthians 9:20-22).*

Paul showed respect by mirroring his audience—adapting his body language, vocabulary, and arguments to their perception of the world. With the cultural differences out of the way, they were able to listen to what he had to say without being distracted. He made them feel comfortable, and he gained their friendship and trust by becoming "like them."

 view

For years, my husband and I enjoyed taking long walks together. He would walk quietly beside me, and I would chatter away, certain he would appreciate an hour-long tour of my thoughts—especially since it included suggestions for how he could improve himself. After a while, I noticed he started going for his walks alone.

A chattering fool comes to ruin (Proverbs 10:8).

When he got around to inviting me along again, I decided to try mirroring him by adapting my conversation style and pace to his. I wasn't sure what that looked like, but I figured if I waited until he spoke before I said anything and kept my responses short and on topic, that would be about as close as I could get to letting him lead the conversation.

The first thing I noticed was how long he could go without saying *anything*. Many walks we didn't speak for the entire hour—which was excruciating for me but apparently enjoyable for him. He even started *waiting* to walk until I could go with him. Once, he was so excited about some news he had received, he talked non-stop the whole time. That incident helped me see what it was like to be on the receiving end of a monologue, but it also made me thankful to know my husband was becoming comfortable enough to share his thoughts with me.

The Alpha Behavior lessons came in handy, too. Instead of dashing between cars ahead of him to cross the street, I began following his lead by waiting until he was ready to go. When we had to walk single file for a passing runner, I stepped behind him, instead of in front of him, unless he invited me to step ahead. Walking side-by-side, I took the side farthest from the street—something I remembered from the old days—so that if a car swerves, he gets it, not me.

Before long, I began to relax, enjoy the scenery, and let him have the responsibility for making all the decisions on our walks. I no longer had to worry that I might do or say something wrong. How could I? I was following him.

The same concepts worked well at the dinner table and in the car. At first, we had long, uncomfortable silences that felt very awkward—but eventually he started opening up and sharing things that were on his mind or heart. What's more, he started truly listening and wanting to know my thoughts on things, as well.

Women don't just *talk* fast, we think fast, too. We think about what we're thinking about, and once we've thought it out thoroughly, we think about it some more. Ironically, we *think* about things to figure out what we want to *say* about them, and we *talk* about things to figure out how we *feel* about them.

We also think about our feelings. Ask any woman what makes her feel loved, for example, and she'll ask you how long you want the list to be. Ask a man the same thing, and he'll give you an off-the-cuff answer or tell you he doesn't know. To him, it's a silly question.

That's not to say men don't think about these things, they just aren't accustomed to keeping track of their thoughts and how they got there. Take this comparison: my husband sees an Italian food advertisement on television, turns to me, and says, "Hey, Italian food would be good tonight." Simple one-two, eyes-to-stomach connection.

I see the same ad and say, "That looks good. Reminds me your prescription is ready." What makes him uncomfortable is not so much that an Italian food advertisement led me to think about his prescription. He's used to that. What bothers him is that I can tell him exactly *how* the connection happened.

"When I saw the ad," I explained, "it reminded me of the trip we took to Italy for your birthday, which made me realize my sister Lori's birthday is just around the corner. Yesterday, she told me her daughter, Randal, wants to study pharmacology, and *that* made me think about your prescription. By the way, since the drugstore is near the Italian restaurant where Nancy works, can we eat at that one? We can save gas—and speaking of saving gas—can you believe Jessica saves four cents a gallon by using that company on the corner? We should start going there."

All he had wanted to do was eat dinner.

 G8 80

Our habit of analyzing makes it very difficult for us to take our husbands at face value. If they're grumpy, we want to know *why*—and what it means.

Kaylin: *(Noticing her husband has been rather distant, lately)* "What's bothering you?"
Caden: "Nothing."
Kaylin: "Are you mad at me or something?"
Caden: "No."
Kaylin: *(Running through a checklist of all the things he could possibly be angry at her for.)* "You're not mad about that dress I bought the other day, are you?"
Caden: "No."
Kaylin: *(Wondering if he just needs some attention)* "Do you want to go to a movie?"
Caden: "Not today."
Kaylin: "Hey, I'll fix your favorite dinner tonight!"
Caden: *(Distant)* "That's nice."
Kaylin: *(After a pause)* "I wish you'd tell me what's wrong."
Caden: "NOTHING'S wrong."
Kaylin: "Then why are you being so distant?"
Caden: "I'm *not* being distant."
Kaylin: "Yes you are. I can tell."

Caden: *(Frustrated)* "NO, I'm not. What's the matter with you?"

Kaylin: *(Convinced it's either the dress, or he's noticed the extra pounds she put on that week.)* "I don't see why you have to be so cold. All I did was buy one dress that I really needed." *(Tears coming to her eyes because she feels overweight.)* "I have nothing to wear that fits, and when was the last time I bought myself something? It was on sale and it cost a lot less than the new gear you bought for yourself."

Caden: "What are you talking about?" *(Are all women this crazy, or just the one I'm married to?)*

Kaylin: *(Crying, angry)* "Don't shut me out. I want to talk about this." *(Getting scared)* "Can't we just talk?"

Caden: *(Angry, frustrated)* "There's nothing to talk about."

Caden may actually have an idea what's bothering him, but that doesn't mean he's analyzed the hows and whys of it enough to talk about it. Certainly not to her, with her mind that's like a trap, never letting anything go until it's thoroughly analyzed and resolved. That's definitely not *his* idea of how he wants to spend the evening—especially since he knows it's not likely to end well.

To her, his refusal to analyze is torture. When a woman hears, "There's nothing to talk about," it means the relationship is in *serious* jeopardy. *Friends* can talk about anything. "Nothing is wrong" means there must be a big something lurking somewhere . . . and she has to figure out what it is.

In fact, when *she* says, "Nothing," what she actually means is, "I expect you to *insist* that I tell you what's wrong, so

I don't feel like such a mean person for having to tell you." Unfortunately, applying what she wants to her husband pushes him into a corner he doesn't want to be in.

CB BO

A husband's moods are like the weather. If it's sunny, he thinks, *"Hey, it's nice outside,"* grabs the golf clubs, motorcycle helmet, or fishing rod and heads out. If it's raining, he thinks, *"Hmm, it's raining,"* and grabs the remote control, instead. He may want it to be sunny again, but he doesn't spend time trying to figure out why it's not or out how to change it back. He just sits down and changes the channel. In the same way, if he's unhappy, he may want to be happy, but he doesn't try to "fix" his moods—and you shouldn't either. Once the clouds go away and the sun comes back out, he'll come looking for you.

Resist the temptation to hound him for assurances of his love or soothe him with assurances of yours. Don't ask a lot of questions or try to "talk about it." You'll only annoy him. Men prefer to keep their unpleasant thoughts separate from the pleasant feelings they have about their wives, and that's a good thing. So don't press the issue.

It's natural to assume he's upset with you, but it's more likely something else like his golf score, the car that has a problem, the finances, or something at work. Even if it *is* something about you, you're better off not making an issue out of it. He'll probably get over it and forget about it—at least until the next time. If there's something *really* serious on his mind, you won't have to ask, it will come out. Bringing it to a head when he doesn't want to talk about only leads to conflict and disagreement, making the problem worse.

Instead, when he's being quiet, recognize it's his way of telling you, *"This is what I need,"* and mirror him by being quiet, also. As strange as that may sound, it feels like respect to him. His body language is your best clue for how he feels, and since you can't read his mind, gently mirroring only as much affection as he shows you is the most reliable way to stay in his range of comfort.

That won't be comfortable because you're a woman, and women want to fix things. Immediately. You're going to have to lean on the Lord for comfort and assurance and pray through your fear or anxiety. If you feel you must talk to him, be sure to pray first—for yourself to choose your words wisely and for him to have a listening heart.

You might be thinking that mirroring sounds manipulative or self-demeaning; but it's less so than trying to draw your husband out of his funk with the usual song and dance routine. It's respectful—and it works. Sooner or later, he'll pull out of his bad mood and be back to his normal, easy-going self.

On the other hand, if you push him to tell you what's wrong when he doesn't want to talk about it, he might just look at your worried face in front of his, forget what was bothering him, and think, *"Hey, this isn't very pleasant. Maybe* she's *the reason I'm unhappy."* That isn't a connection you want him to make.

CB BOCB BO

Chapter 12 - Suggested Prayers

Prayer for You

Father God,

It's so hard when my husband is withdrawn. I can't help but worry that he's disappointed or angry with me. Help me remember, as hard as it is, that it might be more loving to let him work through his feelings privately, than try to get him to talk about them. Give me the strength and courage to be unafraid, prayerful, and patient; and have the confidence to *be still and know that You are God* (from Psalm 46:10).

When we do talk, remind me that the speed of my conversation may shut him off from listening to me. Help me remember to slow down my own pace and mirror his, being willing and sensitive to follow his lead. Soften his heart to hear Your voice, and bless his leadership over our family. In the name of Jesus. Amen.

Prayer to Give to Your Husband

Father God,

Help me have patience with my wife, especially in our communication. Remind me to tell her what I need from her, so she won't be afraid or confused. Open my ears to hear Your voice and teach me to *be still and know that You are God* (from Psalm 46:10). In the name of Jesus. Amen.

Chapter 12 - Homework

1. Who does most of the talking in your home and who leads the conversations? Observe for several days and then ask your husband (and children) what they think. Note your observations.

2. Memorize Proverbs 10:8. Give one example of how you applied it in your life this week

3. As an experiment, let your husband lead your conversations. Don't say anything to him unless he speaks first, keep your responses short and on topic, try to reflect back to him what he says before adding new information, and announce topic changes. Describe one conversation and the results.

4. Describe a situation this week when your husband was withdrawn and bothered by something. What idea from this chapter did you implement? How difficult was it? Was it fear or love that motivated you before? Which one motivates you now?

13. Quiet Companionship

When we make decisions and judgments based on personal standards for right or wrong, it's like viewing the world in a warped mirror—a mirror twisted by private fears and desires. What we see is an image that may be comforting or frightening, but it's not accurate.

It's like standing at the carnival—one person in front of the mirror that makes people look tall and thin, another in front of the one that makes them look short and heavy—each trying to convince the other their image is right. When they try to show us what *we* look like to *them,* we protest, "That isn't me!"

Close your eyes, and you can easily picture the details of your husband's face; but you probably can't picture the details of your *own* face as easily, even though you look at it in the mirror every day. It's the same way with sin: you can see his, but not your own—even when you think you can.

For a while, I worked out of the house during a period when my husband was also home between assignments. There was a big difference, though, in how we each viewed what "being home" meant. I thought it meant getting up at the crack of dawn to tackle the long and growing list of things I had to do.

He thought it meant sleeping late in the morning, reading, eating, checking e-mail, maybe getting a golf game in, and watching television.

I was desperately trying to find more hours in the day to get everything done; he was asking where the remote control was. I was stunned. Even though most of the things on my list weren't actually his responsibility, they were for our joint benefit. How could he not care enough to help me? If the tables had been turned, I would have helped him.

> *How long will you lie there, you sluggard? When will you get up from your sleep? (Proverbs 6:9)*

That and other verses were going through my head—though maybe not in such biblical language. *"Surely my husband's behavior isn't pleasing to you, God,"* I demanded. I had been working hard to stay focused on giving him leadership opportunities, but how was I supposed to follow the lead of someone who's still in bed?

"You stay in bed with them."

"Well, that's a pretty stupid idea," I said to God. It wasn't a pleasant one, either. I had far too much to do to waste time lying around. However, my bitterness was growing, and I had to do something.

Everything else in my submission journey had gone so well, I decided to try it. I would mirror his activity level for thirty days. I'd be lying if I said my motives were entirely pure. Part of me was thinking, *"Maybe he'll get with the program when he sees things don't get done by themselves."*

13. Quiet Companionship

At 5:00 AM the next morning, I woke up and lay very still next to my husband. By the time I could make out the bedposts in the growing light, I was getting nervous. There were so many things I needed to be doing. 7:00 AM. The school bus and the garbage truck went by. *"How can he sleep so soundly?"* I thought, as I lifted up slightly to look at the clock: 8:30 AM. I dropped my head back on the pillow. My body ached.

I prayed and studied the ceiling, trying to figure out how I could tape Bible verses up there to memorize them. I wondered whether or not it would be cheating to read a book, if I read it laying down. By 10:00 AM, I thought I was going to die. There was *no way* anyone could stay in bed this long. Any longer, and I was afraid I would lose my identity in "nothingness" and become *just like him.* I had too much to do, to let that happen.

"Lord," I prayed, *"This was Your idea, and I'm just trying to be obedient. So You're going to have to figure out a way to take care of all those things that need to be done."*

Finally, at 11:00 AM my husband got up. Without saying a word, I got up, too, acting as if it were the most natural thing in the world. I felt like I had just been freed from prison.

I continued to mirror him throughout the day. After a quiet walk together, he went to his study to watch television, so I sat in the den and read a book. When he got up and did a household chore, so did I; when he stopped, I did, too. It was scary to think of the things that weren't getting done; and yet, there was a delicious sort of intrigue about it. It was like being on vacation without leaving home.

By the end of the first week, my annoyance had turned to curiosity. Mirroring his level of activity by letting him set the standard for how hard we worked had made him the leader. For the first time, I didn't feel like I was working harder than he was. In fact, I was hardly working. It was nearly impossible to feel resentful anymore.

As the month progressed, I adjusted to the slower pace and realized he wasn't irresponsible and lazy after all. He just had a different standard of busyness, and it wasn't necessarily wrong. I had stepped into his world and was starting to see the advantages of not rushing around seventeen hours a day, six or seven days a week.

I also realized I didn't have to fill time simply because there was time to fill. Having nothing to do was not a sin. So many of my deadlines had been self-imposed or artificial, put there to keep me on pace. Maybe I had been running from something, or maybe being busy had made me feel important. I think I had just been scared that life might pass me by.

"As soon as I'm finished, I'll spend some time with you," I used to say to my husband. *"Promise. Can you wait just one more hour—I mean a day—sorry it's been three, I know. Well, maybe next week, for sure. Yes, you really are important to me, it's just that I have all these other important things I have to do. You understand."* Busyness had become my priority, and spending time together, the exception; even though I pretended it was the other way around.

It had seemed incomprehensible, when I started the month of mirroring, that I would be able to get anything done in so little time, but I was surprised. Less important things fell by the wayside; the rest I prioritized and got done more quickly because my mind was clearer and more focused. I still have a huge box of things that need to be filed, but I'll get to it someday. I haven't missed anything in it, yet.

Toward the end of the month, my husband announced we were wasting our lives away in bed and started getting us up several hours earlier. I suppose since I had quit trying to be overbearing with my example, he felt free to move into more responsibility without looking like he was obeying me. He was taking the lead.

CS ᘓᗴ

When my husband read the first draft of this book, he started laughing when he got to this chapter. Unbelievably, he had never noticed I had been mirroring him all those weeks. That says volumes about the difference in what we each had thought was important, and it also explains why he had never seemed to appreciate all the things I did for us in the past. I had been moving so fast and doing so much, I had been just a blur of activity to him—a blur that said, *"I'm too busy to spend time with you."*

The most important thing I learned during that experiment was what made my husband happy. He didn't care if we had a perfectly clean home or I completed a remarkable work project. What meant the most to him was simply having me quietly in his presence.

I realize staying in bed late is not practical for most households. You need to go to work; there are children and pets to tend to; or your husband is an early-riser, and you're not.

However, there are other ways to look for moments to share Quiet Companionship.

In the evening, for example, my husband and I usually end up in separate rooms: he watches television in one, and I listen to music and read in another. Inevitably, at some point, I feel guilty for ignoring him—or I worry that he's ignoring me.

I used to go into his study and announce, "We need to spend more time together; let's do something." When that didn't work, I'd sit down next to him and ask questions about the show he was watching. Neither of those approaches was particularly endearing.

Practicing Quiet Companionship, I started going in quietly and sitting close to him. He'd put his arm around me and we'd sit together for a little while, watching the channels change. Then, without a word, I would kiss him good-bye and go back to the den to read. It was such a simple thing, but it seemed to make him feel more loved than a thousand words of affection or praise.

CR ››

Typically, when I share the concepts of Mirroring and Quiet Companionship with other women, they're incredulous. "My husband is not at *all* interested in my companionship!" they declare emphatically. "And besides, I *don't* have time! If he wants to be together so much, where is he? Why doesn't he come do something *I* want to do?"

If they're willing to give it a try, though, they almost always write me later with moving testimonies, like this one:

Yesterday my husband had to fly out at noon and worked from home in the morning rather than go to the office. I had a slew of things to do but when he chose to stay in bed a bit longer, I stayed with him remembering your counsel. I prayed silently to the Lord, surrendering my schedule for the morning.

The morning went well, he left feeling loved—evidenced by a rare and loving phone call before boarding the plane—and everything that needed to be done, was completed. It is hard to make the best choice sometimes, it can be such a battle, but when we choose His best, oh, how sweet the victories are.

Another woman's husband worked four nights of the week away from home—and always found some reason not to be home the other three. When she started practicing Quiet Companionship in the little time they *did* have together, he started making a point to come home. He even stopped by her office, just to say hello, and began inviting her to do things with him. On a scale from one to ten, in her estimation, their relationship had gone from a one to an eight in just weeks.

"Was it worth the effort to take time to exercise Quiet Companionship?" I asked.

"Absolutely," she answered, smiling.

CB ✥

Thinking back over the few really happy couples I've known, I've realized they spend a lot of time quietly being together. The same is proving true for us. The more I practice just being with my husband in Quiet Companionship, the more loving and cheerful he becomes. When I neglect him, he grows grumpy and distant. Amazing. All these years I've been trying to demonstrate my love for him and make him happy, when all I really needed to do was shut my mouth and sit down beside him.

I'll be the first to admit it isn't something I completely understand. *"How could it be meaningful to him for me to lie in bed beside him while he's sleeping? How could it matter if I got up for a little while to work, as long as I returned to bed before he woke?"*

There's no denying the evidence, though. Any time I get up early and work while he sleeps, he's inevitably grouchy the rest of the day—and I doubt he even makes the connection.

One day, I asked my husband what it was about Quiet Companionship that he enjoyed so much.

"I don't know," he said. "It's just nice having you there with me."

I guess it's as simple as that.

08 80 08 80

Chapter 13 - Suggested Prayers

Prayer for You

Heavenly Father,

You are the One and Only God, Creator of all that exists. Nothing exists that You didn't make. Only You are worthy of our praise.

Guide me in setting priorities for my life and my time, so I can achieve a godly balance between work and rest. I don't want to be so busy that I leave no room to spend quiet time with my husband. Give me compassion, kindness, and an open mind to try living according to his levels of activity for a while and see what I might learn. May I never again be so self-righteous that I think only my way is right.

Help me remember the importance of Quiet Companionship and how meeting my husband's unspoken need in this area lets him know how much I love him. In Jesus' name. Amen.

Prayer to Give to Your Husband

Heavenly Father,

Thank you for a wife who works hard. Help me teach her the importance of relaxing and spending quiet time just being together. Give her a clear mind that is able to distinguish between truly important needs and those that just seem important. In Jesus' name. Amen.

Chapter 13 - Homework

1. What are your top five daily priorities? Ask you husband what his are.

2. What are your top five most enjoyable activities? Ask your husband what his are.

3. What five things do you have to do often, that you least enjoy? Ask your husband for his five. Compare.

4. What five things do you enjoy doing and wish you could do more often? Ask your husband for his five. Compare.

5. Spend at least thirty minutes each day just sitting quietly with your husband. Note your observations.

SECTION FOUR

Going Deeper

14. Two Steps Backward

There are times when I don't feel particularly "pious"—when pulling out my Bible, saying grace, or getting on my knees to pray seems like a ritual habit or even a chore. Those are the days when it feels like "too much trouble" to be righteous, and I've slipped into thinking I can be holy in my own strength.

Fortunately, God never lets me get very far down that path before reminding me how much I need Him. What was that verse?

> *Pride goes before destruction, a haughty spirit before a fall (Proverbs 16:18).*

ଔ ଞ

One day, my husband and I had a wonderful morning at church. He was loving and affectionate, and I was on cloud nine. I wasn't aware of being proud, but in retrospect, I probably *was* thinking I had the submission thing down pretty well, and I did feel some pride when someone commented how in love we seemed.

On the way home, my husband suddenly grew critical—and more so with every mile. Not knowing how to respond to his abrupt change of mood, I stared quietly out the window through watery eyes, watching the scenery slip past. Discouragement colored my heart. I had been trying so hard, and we had been doing so well. Now, he was acting like this. Had we come this far only to find ourselves back at square one?

My confidence wavered, and for a moment I doubted God's Word. I had been faithful. Where was my husband's faithfulness? When we got home, I went to another room and lay face down on the floor in tearful prayer. My emotions were a whirl of self-pity, confusion, frustration, and despair.

Help me, Lord. I know you want me to be loving and submissive to his leadership, but I'm so frustrated. Just when I thought we were doing great, he goes back to his old ways. I thought if I did everything right, You would bless us. Why don't You fix him?

I stayed that way for nearly an hour before I had the courage to ask God if there was perhaps a *remote possibility I* had done something wrong. He then showed me the morning from *His* perspective, and I realized I had not only contributed to the situation, I had caused it. All morning, I had focused on what I had wanted to get done and treated my husband like a child tagging along with a busy parent, rather than like the leader of our family. True, he had responded poorly, but that was between him and God. It had been my ungodly actions that had started the downward spiral.

After desire has conceived, it gives birth to sin; and sin, when it is full-grown, gives birth to death (James 1:15).

Within the framework of that verse, completing my "to do" list with maximum efficiency had been my *desire,* and it had taken precedence over honoring God by respecting my husband. Frankly, the only thought I had about God *or* my husband—if I *had* a thought about either of them that morning—was that they would both surely forgive my self-centeredness since I was being so nice about it. My *sin* had been manipulating my husband, willingly taking advantage of his good nature and failing to respect his headship. The *death* had been the pain and destruction caused in our relationship.

It's human nature to put ourselves above reproach, holding a magnifying glass up to another's sin and a flattering mirror up to our own. I certainly hadn't *intended* to neglect the precept of the log and the speck; I had just been peeping out of a knothole in my own log for so long, I hadn't even known it was sticking out both sides of my head.

> *How can you say to your brother, 'Brother, let me take the speck out of your eye,' when you yourself fail to see the plank in your own eye? . . . First take the plank out of your eye, and then you will see clearly to remove the speck from your brother's eye (Luke 6:42).*

Only later did I realize how twisted and self-serving my thinking had become: if I was angry, it was because of *his* unkindness; if he was angry, it was because of *his* immaturity. It was his fault, regardless. My anger was based on how good I thought I was, how I felt I was being dishonored, and what I wanted. That's called unrighteous anger, and it usually points to an idol of the heart.

This is where secular marriage guides—and even some Christian ones—break down. Too often, their focus is on achieving our own happiness, the happiness of our husbands (both of which are formidable tasks), or on simply improving our marriages. Any of these three goals can easily become false gods, or idols, into which we put our trust. Success is only temporary, because trying to attain the blessings of God through our own effort is futile. When things fall apart, unrighteous anger flares up and takes over—inflamed by resentment for the sacrifices we have made ("How could you, after all I've done for you . . . !").

Who can discern her errors? (from Psalm 19:12).

The Bible says our only goal should be "to please God." That means keeping our hearts focused on honoring Him through our obedience; and offering Him thanksgiving and praise for the blessings He deems appropriate to give us. That's much different than deciding what blessings we want and trying to figure out how to get God to give them to us. In actual practice, it's a fine line—one that's often and easily crossed.

CB EO

I was ready to confess and reconcile with my husband. In the past, I would have said something like, "I'm sorry I had so much to do earlier," or "I'm sorry you got so upset with me today." Those might have been true statements, but neither would have expressed responsibility for my own actions nor repentance. They would have just implied I was sorry for the *consequences* that came out of those actions.

An apology takes only one person. It's a statement, not a question, so it's not an interaction. Even if the other person responds, "That's okay," it's not really effective in granting forgiveness. It's sort of like tossing a handful of grain on the altar and hoping it's good enough. There's always a lingering haze of doubt left hanging in the air.

Forgiveness, on the other hand, takes two people: one to ask and one to grant. "Will you forgive me" is a question that begs an answer, like putting your bare neck on the altar and waiting for the other person to accept your sacrifice. The process of forgiveness focuses on the sin itself, rather than the consequences of that sin. It's the biblical way to handle wrongdoing, and it's also the only thing that can truly clear the air and reconcile or restore relationships.

For the sake of your name, O LORD, forgive my iniquity, though it is great (Psalm 25:11).

Convicted and repentant, I walked into my husband's study and said, "I sinned against God and you by disrespecting you this morning. Will you forgive me?"

"It's okay," he said, half an eye on the television.

"No, I really need to ask your forgiveness," I replied.

"I forgive you." he said, turning to look at me. "Will you forgive me?" Those were the sweetest words.

Blessed is she whose transgressions are forgiven, whose sins are covered (from Psalm 32:1).

CB EO

Exactly one week later (God wasn't wasting any time with me) we stopped by the store so I could run in and pick up a few groceries. My husband usually drops me off at the door; then parks who-knows-where to listen to the radio and wait. He seems to think that since *he* knows where he is, *I* must know where he is; because when I tell him I had a hard time finding him, he always says something like, "I was *right here* the whole time." (Silly me. I should have known he was between the white pick-up and the red SUV on the twelfth row, seventh aisle, facing the back of the lot . . . where *else* would he be?)

That day, determined to avoid even the *potential* of a repeat scenario of the week before—godly growth excepted—I asked him in advance where he was going to park. I thought I was pretty smart, turning it into a Moment of Leadership.

"Right there," he said, pointing to the end of a row as he dropped me off.

It was a long way from the door, but I wasn't going to spoil the nice afternoon we had planned, by complaining. I rushed through the store, conscious of the fact he was waiting for me, and emerged a little while later with a dozen heavy plastic bags hanging from my fingers.

By the time I got to where he had said he would be, my godly attitude had evaporated. He was nowhere to be found, and I was furious. I know it was childish, but at the time all I could think about was how I had done everything possible to accommodate him, and he hadn't even done the one thing he had said he would do. It was unrighteous anger.

After ten minutes of looking for him in the hundred-degree summer heat, I thought I saw him pull out of a spot on the far side of the lot. *"If that's him, he can jolly well come find me,"* I thought, as I sat down on a curb in the shade of a small tree. A minute later, he pulled around the end of the row, parked right where he had said he would and jumped out to help take the bags. Clueless of his transgression, he was smiling.

"Don't touch me," I snarled as I practically threw the groceries in the car, surprising myself with my hatefulness. "Where were you?"

"Over there," he said, warily pointing to where I thought I had seen him a dozen rows over, "but you were taking a while, so I decided to come find you."

Who knows *why* he parked somewhere else? He's not a malicious person. Maybe he forgot. Maybe he just didn't realize how important it was to me. Knowing why wouldn't have mattered; there was no excuse as far as I was concerned. Sitting in the car, I mumbled how inconsiderate he had been, he replied it was all my fault, and we fell into a cold silence. The icicles hanging off the bumper probably left gouges in the road.

Once home, I went straight to the couch and sat there, steely and uncaring, leaving the groceries for him to unload. As far as I was concerned, I had a *right* to be angry this time and wasn't about to offer him an apology or ask for his forgiveness. He owed *me* some godly attitude. The door to his study slammed shut, and I rolled my eyes, *"Whatever."* I was tired of trying to please God all the time. Let God could work on *him* for a while. Unrighteous anger.

Silence.

The more I thought about how much I had been looking forward to a great afternoon together—and how he had spoiled it—the angrier I got.

Silence.

I didn't feel like praying, either. The day was ruined, my walk with the Lord was tarnished, and it was *his fault*.

Silence.

I remembered a book I hadn't read yet on how to handle anger biblically, so I pulled it off the shelf, only half inspired. *"At least reading it while I'm actually angry might be interesting,"* I muttered.

It described two parts of anger—the anger itself, and the way we handle it—and said we could displease God in one or the other, or both.[14] I considered that for a few minutes. I wasn't willing to relinquish my anger, but I did feel bad for acting so hatefully. I could sincerely ask his forgiveness for that, at least. It was a small step, but it was *something*.

My heart immediately began to soften—not so much toward my husband, at first, but toward God. It was like moving out of the shade into the sun on a cold day and turning my face toward the warmth. With every step I took toward my husband's study, my desire to please God grew stronger.

"I'm not capable of honestly asking your forgiveness for being angry right now," I said as I sat down next to him, "but I do want to ask your forgiveness for the way I handled that anger. I was hateful, and that was wrong. Will you forgive me?"

He coolly acknowledged he would—but didn't ask for my forgiveness in return. Oddly enough, it didn't bother me. His anger was between him and God, not me.

If I had asked for his forgiveness in order to get him to ask for mine in return, I would have been resentful when he hadn't done so. But my baby step of obedience to God had given me inexplicable peace. I shouldn't have been surprised. It is, after all, what He promises:

> *Do not be anxious about anything, but in everything, by prayer and petition, with thanksgiving, present your requests to God. And the peace of God, which transcends all understanding, will guard your hearts and minds in Christ Jesus (Philippians 4:6-7).*

My unrighteous anger had come from making myself into a god and putting that god-self on the throne of my heart. When I repented and turned my focus from pleasing my god-self to pleasing the one true God again, the rightful King took His place on the throne of my heart and His sovereign power caused my anger to fall like broken chains to the floor. I was set free. I wasn't even angry at my husband anymore.

> *If my people, who are called by my name, will humble themselves and pray and seek my face and turn from their wicked ways, then will I hear from heaven and will forgive their sin and will heal their land (2 Chronicles 7:14).*

CB EO

My goal in life, as I stumbled through relationships and marriages, had been to avoid conflict and find a man who "fit" me perfectly—someone who would make me happy. Never mind that I couldn't see my own faults and he couldn't see his. In my fantasy, we'd be like two rough stones, our imperfections fitting perfectly together, interlocked in harmony as we sat side-by-side in the sun, happily ever after.

But marriage is more like a rock tumbler—a place where two people bounce around together, knocking the rough edges off each other, and being sanded smooth by the grit of the Holy Spirit. It's one of God's most important tools for making men and women more holy, and it's not easy. But it is glorious.

> *No discipline seems pleasant at the time, but painful. Later on, however, it produces a harvest of righteousness and peace for those who have been trained by it (Hebrews 12:11).*

If you don't understand that, you will inevitably want to escape when marriage gets hard, hoping to find someone else who will make you less angry or less irritable. Someone, in other words, who will bring out less of your sin.

That kind of thinking betrays a lack of understanding of God's ways. He doesn't allow you to have struggles in your marriage because He wants to harm you. He allows them because He knows exactly what you need in order to reveal the sins and idols you can't see in yourself, overcome them, and share more greatly in His joy and fellowship. [15]

> *"I know the plans I have for you," declares the LORD, "plans to prosper you and not to harm you, plans to give you hope and a future" (Jer. 29:11).*

You can run from God, but you can't hide. Take it from a woman who's tried. No matter how far you go, He will never stop pursuing you and drawing you into His holiness process.

CB BOCB BO

Chapter 14 ~ Suggested Prayers

Prayer for You

Lord,

You alone are holy and righteous. Help me see that when I am angry, I'm protecting the idols of my heart and worshipping myself or my false gods. Reveal those idols to me, so I may confess and repent of them. Give me the courage to ask for forgiveness instead of just giving apologies.

Bless our marriage by turning our eyes toward You. Forgive me for my sins of self-righteousness and pride, not only with my husband, but also with You. Too many times, I have resisted the changes you wanted me to make in me, by pridefully managing my disappointment, rather than humbly letting it reveal the sins in my heart.

Give me the desire to be pleasing to You. May I have wisdom to recognize my sins and the grace to ask my husband to forgive me when I've sinned against him. I love you, Lord. Thank You for loving me enough to discipline me so I may grow in fellowship with You. In Jesus' name. Amen.

Prayer to Give to Your Husband

Lord,

Help us remember to worship only You, as worshipping anything else leads to destruction. Give us the humility to ask for forgiveness from each other when we have sinned. In Jesus' name. Amen.

Chapter 14 ~ Homework

1. Fill in this blank: "If only _____, then I would be happy."[16] (Your answer is a clue to your idols.)

2. List the thoughts you have most often throughout the day about your husband. Do the same for the thoughts you have about yourself. How are they related to what you believe you need in order to be happy?

3. What makes you angry? Is there a connection between your anger and the feeling of being dishonored or being denied something you feel is important? Give an example of how that might drive you to behave in an ungodly way.

4. Give an example of setting aside your anger, in order to honor God through obedience

5. Memorize James 1:15 and give several examples of specific desires can lead to sin and destruction. Find three times this week to share that verse with someone else in a practical way that helps them.

6. Ask your husband's forgiveness for something this week, framing your request for that forgiveness in terms of the sin committed against God—not the consequences.

15. Guilty as Charged

"**I**'m sorry," is such an overused phrase. We say it to soothe hurt feelings, to admit guilt, and especially to avoid punishment. However, we also use it as a weapon. When someone says, "I'm sorry, but I'm filing for divorce, no matter what you say," it's hardly godly remorse. It's an expression of a *lack* of sorrow, a way of saying nothing will cause that person to change their mind. Other times it's a desperate plea, "Please don't leave, I *said* I was sorry!" or a sarcastic defense, "Fine, I'm sorry, happy now?"

Then there's, "I feel so guilty." What exactly does that mean? "I'm embarrassed," maybe. "I hope you don't hate me," possibly. "I wish I could hide out somewhere for a while," probably. These are expressions of regret, but they don't provide restoration or reconciliation because they're *false* guilt.[17]

False guilt has no conscience, zero foresight, and will sleep right through sin if it can—waking just enough to pull the covers up and hit the snooze button. It only comes fully awake when there's a threat of negative consequences for sinful actions or words, and its main concern is to avoid those consequences. Adam and Eve were the first to evidence false guilt; and ever since, people have hidden, lied, blame-shifted, or blurred the truth to try and escape the consequences of sin.

> *Then the man and his wife heard the sound of the LORD God as he was walking in the garden in the cool of the day, and they hid from the LORD God among the trees of the garden. But the LORD God called to the man, "Where are you?"*
>
> *He answered, "I heard you in the garden, and I was afraid because I was naked; so I hid."* [Hiding]
>
> *And he said, "Who told you that you were naked? Have you eaten from the tree that I commanded you not to eat from?"*
>
> *The man said, "The woman you put here with me— she gave me some fruit from the tree, and I ate it."* [Shifting blame to Eve]
>
> *Then the LORD God said to the woman, "What is this you have done?"*
>
> *The woman said, "The serpent deceived me, and I ate."* [Shifting blame and blurring the truth.] *(Genesis 3:8-13 with inserted notes)*

On the other hand, *true* guilt is given by God to warn us when we are in sin. It is intended to make us stop, grieve for how we have dishonored Him, and repent. When we don't, it sticks to our souls like soot.

> *Nothing in all creation is hidden from God's sight. Everything is uncovered and laid bare before the eyes of him to whom we must give account (Hebrews 4:13).*

True guilt may seem like a curse, but it's actually a blessing. It doesn't make something right or wrong; it gives us the ability to distinguish the difference—and forces us to make a choice. It *never* gives up on us. It never stops trying to bring us back into fellowship with God. Like fingernails scratching across a blackboard, it *will* get our attention.

The sacrifice and resurrection of Jesus are the confidence by which we know we can be delivered from the pressing sense of true guilt. Through Him we can be forgiven; and through His Holy Spirit living in us, we can have the wisdom and strength to stand against sin. That doesn't mean we won't be tempted, but it does mean we have the potential to overcome.

CB EO

Several years ago, there was a man I worked with who liked to joke around with light-hearted, personal banter—not sexual innuendos, just friendliness—and I enjoyed the diversion. As I was getting ready for work one day, though, I noticed the subtlest change: I caught myself wondering if my co-worker would like the outfit I had chosen to wear.

True guilt immediately set off an alarm, telling me I was dishonoring God and my marriage with those thoughts. False guilt, which is only concerned with consequences, said, *"It's not a big deal to enjoy a little flirtation; it's just harmless fun. You're not doing anything wrong. Relax."*

A battle was going on inside my heart and mind, and even though I was a born-again believer and follower of Jesus, I found myself cheering for the wrong side.

For the sinful nature desires what is contrary to the Spirit, and the Spirit what is contrary to the sinful nature. They are in conflict with each other, so that you do not do what you want (Galatians 5:17).

Knowing Jesus doesn't mean we won't still struggle to do what we should. Paul, who wrote much of the New Testament, says this about himself:

I do not understand what I do. For what I want to do I do not do, but what I hate I do. I have the desire to do what is good, but I cannot carry it out. No, the evil I do not want to do—this I keep on doing.

In my inner being I delight in God's law; but I see another law at work in the members of my body, waging war against the law of my mind and making me a prisoner of the law of sin at work within my members. What a wretched man I am! Who will rescue me from this body of death? Thanks be to God—through Christ Jesus our Lord! (from Romans 7:15-25).

It's easy to relate to Paul's agony and the dizzying, torturous struggle against personal temptation. Satan uses the same scripts over and over because they work, tempting us away from the Holy Spirit by appealing to our flesh nature. His goal is for us to lose our balance and fall headlong into the snare of sin and unconfessed true guilt, which causes us to turn from our Lord, toward self-destruction.

15. Guilty as Charged

I had been in Satan's web before and didn't want to go there again. With every ounce of will power I could muster, I grabbed onto the tiny desire I had to obey God—an infinitesimal seed of faith, compared to the mountain of temptation to keep enjoying my sin. I literally forced myself to kneel right there in the bathroom and asked Jesus to help me turn back toward God.

In one of the most incredible experiences I have ever had, it was like spiritual scales fell from my eyes. The temptation, which had seemed so overpowering a second before, vanished instantly as though it had only been smoke and mirrors.

If you have faith as small as a mustard seed, you can say to this mountain, 'Move from here to there' and it will move (Matthew 17:18).

Miraculously, that small bit of faith was all God had needed to unleash His power in my life. When I clung to it in His name, the "mountains" moved, and what had been impossible in my own strength was brought to nothing by the Holy Spirit.

You, dear children are from God and have overcome them, because the one who is in you is greater than the one who is in the world (1 John 4:4).

The temptation to flirt has not returned since—not because I count on myself to resist it, but because I know in my own strength, I *can't*. It is only by letting the Holy Spirit have free reign in my heart that I am kept from falling.

So, if you think you are standing firm, be careful that you don't fall! (1 Corinthians 10:12).

Sin always causes you to justify your actions and deceives you into thinking you're an exception and your situation is unique. You're not—and it's not. When you hear the voice of Satan whispering, *"It's fun and no one's getting hurt;" "You can't help it, it's not your fault;" "It feels right, so it must be right;"* or *"You're unhappy, you deserve better;"* don't be fooled. Ask God to open your eyes and reveal the truth.

Admit you're human and put in place ways to protect yourself in the areas where your personality, your work, and your environment make you most vulnerable to Satan's lies. Set up protections and parameters *before* you slip into the stupid, blind, foolishness that comes from sin, and you will prevent much agony and heartbreak.

If you do what is right, will you not be accepted? But if you do not do what is right, sin is crouching at your door; it desires to have you, but you must master it (Genesis 4:7).

For my husband and me, protecting ourselves took the form of an agreement. We were executives at the time we met, and knew from experience that when co-workers or clients spend repeated time alone, it often leads to sin. Conversations turn personal and, sooner or later, a disappointment or hurt is shared. Once that emotional bond is built, it can easily become the first step to lust, self-deception, deceit, and even adultery.

Therefore, our written agreement—or *covenant* as we called it, to reflect our desire to please God—said that neither of us would regularly meet with the same person of the opposite sex, alone. It wasn't a difficult thing to honor. We simply invited someone else along whenever we found ourselves in that situation. Sometimes, it even created an opportunity to explain our covenant, the commonality of sin, and the universal need for Christ.

We also agreed our personal Internet account information and passwords would not be secret; briefcases, purses, or journals would not be off-limits; and we would give each other standing permission to directly address concerns. Our desire to hold each other accountable was not based on lack of trust, but on our understanding of the sinful tendencies of human nature and our mutual hope for a long, godly marriage.

Having that covenant in place has been one of the best things we have ever done. It's a constant reminder to us of how important it is to be diligent in protecting ourselves against Satan's wiles, and a public witness of our desire to be obedient to God. Neither of us wants the other to be separated from Him.

CB EO

It's tempting to insist, *"I'd never do that,"* when hearing about someone else's sins; but if David, a "man after God's own heart" and the ancestor of Jesus could fall into terrible sin, you and your husband could, too. No matter how good your intentions, no matter how committed you are to your marriage, you still need God's Holy Spirit to stand firm. You cannot fight yourself in your own strength and win.

Watch and pray, lest you enter into temptation. The spirit indeed is willing (to resist), but the flesh is weak (Mark 14:38 NKJV).

Maybe the temptation you struggle with is not flirting. Maybe it's overeating, busyness, laziness, depression, anger, pornography, alcohol, self-harm, or unwise spending. One of Satan's favorite ploys is to distract you with both *false guilt* and *desire* in your area of weakness, so they feed off each other, dominating your thoughts and paralyzing your spiritual walk.

Since your husband is the spiritual leader of your family, ask him to pray for you in the specific area with which you struggle. Instead of defending yourself or complaining, say:

I confess I'm not leaning on the Holy Spirit in this area of my life. I'm trying to fight sin and temptation with my own strength and I need your help. As the spiritual leader of our home, please pray that I give the Holy Spirit full reign in my heart, putting off the temptation to sin in this area, and putting on a desire to please God.

Cover your husband in prayer, too, that he may be protected from temptation and have the strength to resist sin through the power of the Holy Spirit. When sinful desires ensnare him, pray for his heart to be so convicted, he will immediately turn away. It's not about fear or control. It's about loving him enough to invest in daily prayer time on his behalf, which is the most important thing you can do for him and for your marriage.

15. Guilty as Charged

Confess your sins to each other and pray for each other so that you may be healed. The prayer of a righteous man is powerful and effective (James 5:16).

છ ૪૦

Before I was saved, my understanding of sin could have been compared to standing outside on a moonlit night in the city. The lights of my idols were so bright I could only see a few stars, representing my sins. Anyone else would have known there were more, but I wouldn't have believed it, because I couldn't have seen them for myself. "I'm a pretty good person," I would have said as I looked upward. "Sure, I've got some faults here and there, but overall, I'm not so bad. Lovely night."

For in her own eyes she flatters herself too much to detect or hate her sin (from Psalm 36:2).

When I asked Jesus into my life, it was like He took me from the city with its lights, to the country, where the stars revealed themselves across the dark sky. He showed me sins I hadn't been able to see—so many they were beyond counting. If I *thought* I had needed His grace before, now I *knew* it, and I clung to Him with passion and conviction.

Where sin increased, grace increased all the more (Romans 5:20b).

As my faith grew, God increased my vision even more, allowing me to see myself—at least to a degree—as He saw me.

Lifting me from that spot in the country, He took me to a spiritual *Hubble telescope* and showed me how many of those individual stars were actually other galaxies, and beyond that, giant nebulae constantly churning out new stars.

It was a stark realization: I wasn't a "pretty good person with a few sins" or even a "fairly decent person with millions of sins covered by Christ." I was an endless universe of sin, limited only by my ability or willingness to perceive them.

> *I know that nothing good lives in me, that is, in my sinful nature (Romans 7:18).*

No matter how "good" I became, I would never be truly good—not in my own strength. The more I progressed, the farther out the goal would move. For every sin I acknowledged, confessed, and overcame, my sensitivity to the Holy Spirit in perceiving my sin would increase that much more. In that wisdom, I finally understood the fear of the Lord and the immeasurability of God's goodness.

> *Then you will understand the fear of the LORD and find the knowledge of God (Proverbs 2:5).*

Without the hope and salvation of Jesus Christ in my life, God's continuing revelation of my sinful nature would have led me into despair beyond imagining. With the sanctifying power of Christ in my heart, however, the more I grasped the depth of my sin, the more my gratitude and love for Him increased—and the more joyful and confident I became in my faith.

Through truly understanding my sin, I came to truly understand my salvation.

Therefore, I tell you, she who has been forgiven much, loves much. But she who has been forgiven little, loves little (my adaptation of Luke 7:47).

Being delivered from sinful desire is only part of the process of becoming more like Christ. Without an adequate understanding of the depth of our sin nature, our prayer life can easily become dominated by requests for God to remove our sinful desires (or change our husbands) in order that we might find it *easier* to be more righteous and obedient.

What He has called us to do is something harder. He has called us to make continual sacrifices of those desires, laying ourselves on the cross of obedience, in faith—even when every ounce of our flesh wants to do otherwise.

Jesus sweat blood in the Garden of Gethsemane as He prepared to submit Himself to the Father's will—and He was perfectly good. Why should we expect it to be easier for us?

If anyone would come after me, she must deny herself and take up her cross and follow me (from Matthew 16:24).

CB ED CB ED

Chapter 15 ~ Suggested Prayers

Prayer for You

Dear God,

You are so wonderful, so amazing, so loving. I praise You for all that You are. Thank You for giving me life. Thank You for my husband and for filling my heart with love for him. I want to worship only You, God. May the Holy Spirit convict me when I sin and give me the strength to overcome. Help me become more like Jesus.

Holy is Your Name, Father. Forgive me as I forgive others and lead me not into temptation, but deliver me from evil. You will help me overcome if I am willing. I give you my will and ask You to deliver me specifically from the temptation of _____. Show me how to replace sinful behavior in this area with active, godly behavior. I ask not for ease, but for strength. For Yours is the kingdom and the power and the glory, forever. Amen.

Prayer to Give to Your Husband

Lord,

Bless my wife. I know that sin separates us from You. Give my wife strength today to resist temptation, specifically in the area of_____. Help her trust in You. In Jesus' name. Amen.

Chapter 15 - Homework

1. What sin(s) do you struggle the most with?

2. Write out a sample "inner dialogue" you have with yourself when you are tempted in sin.

3. Briefly describe false guilt and true guilt, giving an example of each in your life.

4. Keep your journal by your bed for a week. Make a list of the things that preoccupy your mind as you lay in bed before rising in the morning and before going to sleep at night. Summarize your findings. Look for false guilt-desire battles. How can you frame your sin in terms of true guilt, instead?

5. Memorize Genesis 4:7 and explain it to two people this week in a way that helps them through a situation they are struggling with. Write their names, the date, time, and circumstances—as well as their reaction.

6. What sin have you asked God to remove your desire for? How long have you struggled with that sin? Ask your husband to pray for you to sacrifice those desires and lean on the Holy Spirit in that area.

16. Suitable Helper

The Hebrew word used when God describes woman as man's "helper" is `ezer, and every other time that word appears in the Bible, it refers to the LORD God helping—always in affiliation with words such as sword, shield, deliverer, salvation, and hope.

> The LORD God said, "It is not good for the man to be alone. I will make a helper suitable for him" (Genesis 2:18).

> My father's God was my helper; he saved me from the sword of Pharaoh (Exodus 18:4).

> Hear, O LORD, the cry of Judah . . . Oh, be his help against his foes! (Deuteronomy 33:7).

> Who is like you, a people saved by the LORD? He is your shield and helper and your glorious sword (Deuteronomy 33:29).

> We wait in hope for the LORD; he is our help and our shield (Psalm 33:20).

You are my help and my deliverer; O LORD, do not delay (Psalm 70:5).

I lift up my eyes to the hills—where does my help come from? My help comes from the LORD (Psalm 121:1, 2).

Blessed is he whose help is the God of Jacob whose hope is in the LORD his God (Psalm 146:5).

Clearly, 'ezer does not refer to someone who is subservient, weak, or inferior; but strong, powerful, and uniquely suited to the need at hand. As your husband's helper, God wants you to *use* your gifts of strength and intelligence, not forfeit them to become a mindless slave who anticipates and satisfies her husband's every need. That kind of thinking just helps a man become an *ungodly* leader who is slothful, lazy, self-centered, and demanding.

You are called to *be* the crown on your husband's head, not *put* one on it:

A wife of noble character is her husband's crown (Proverbs 12:4).

 C3 80

In the second chapter of Genesis, God created woman only after looking all over the earth and determining that no suitable helper could be found for man:

16. Suitable Helper

For Adam no suitable helper was found. So the LORD God caused the man to fall into a deep sleep; and while he was sleeping, he took one of the man's ribs and closed up the place with flesh. Then the LORD God made a woman from the rib he had taken out of the man, and he brought her to the man (Genesis 2:20-22).

When I ask women how they help their husbands, most say they cook, clean the house, raise the children, and provide physical companionship. Some help with their husband's business. These are all fine and good, and they *are* helpful; but they're needs filled as easily by a cook, a housekeeper, a nanny, a friend, or an employee.

God created Eve for a purpose so unique and so important that nothing else in all of creation would ever be able to fill it for Adam. She was bone of his bones and flesh of his flesh (Genesis 2:23). Only she would know him intimately enough to be his *spiritual* helper; and only she could provide the means for him to be a godly leader by choosing to follow him.

But Eve denied Adam's leadership and spiritual covering: she followed her own ways, apart from God, and then invited Adam to follow *her* leadership. It is for this—*not* her recipe for wild boar, her farming skills, or the way she raised her sons— that we remember her. And it is this legacy which she left us.

03 80

By now, hopefully you're experiencing how empowering, fun, and easy practicing Active Submission and Moments of Leadership can be. They're empowering because they give you the ability to create openings for your husband to grow and change in areas you might have thought were hopeless. They're fun because you get to see God in action, up close, from a seat at the fifty-yard line. They're easy because you choose the situations in which you're willing to step back and give your husband opportunities to lead.

However, there are times when it's not so easy or fun—when situations you don't choose to have happen leave you feeling victimized or angry. Your heart pounds, you rage inside, and your take-charge instincts go into high gear. How can you be an active spiritual helper to your husband when what you really want to do is show him the door?

You have three choices: bury your feelings and act happy, attack and control, or forgive and forget. The first is deceitful, the second is destructive, and the third is difficult. Forgiveness and restoration are God's commands, but how do you get there?

If you do nothing, you're actually helping your husband be an ungodly leader, and he'll treat you with contempt and disregard. If you lecture him on what he did wrong, you're taking the lead by trying to be his conscience, and he'll tune you out. Then, when he hears the voice of his own conscience, he'll confuse it with yours and tune it out, too.

If you pretend to forgive him when your heart is still bitter, you're being deceitful. You'll cause yourself great pain and hurt the marriage because he won't respond as you hoped he would. Then you'll be angry for having sacrificed yourself to the idol of his love, without the desired blessing.

Each of these is an attempt to handle the situation in a way that satisfies your need to avoid his anger or vent your own. They're not really God-pleasing. What God asks of you is something much more interesting: harder because it's not familiar, but easier because it's so effective. God asks you to hold your husband accountable for his actions—without taking leadership—and leave room for the Holy Spirit to do what He does best.

CB EO

My husband and I were working with a number of people at the church one afternoon when he barked out a harsh, sarcastic demand for me to do something. Everyone in the room quickly pretended to be preoccupied with other things.

Admittedly, it wasn't a big deal, but it was embarrassing. His command hung awkwardly in the air, and it was impossible to pretend I hadn't heard. How could I respond in a way that would let him know he had spoken wrongly, without giving way to unrighteous anger?

A gentle answer turns away wrath, but a harsh word stirs up anger (Proverbs 15:1).

Remembering the punch line from a humorous story I had heard years earlier, I said, "I know you meant that in a nice way." Then I did what he had asked. There were a few chuckles, everyone relaxed, and the incident was soon forgotten. I had helped my husband by holding him accountable—without being disrespectful—and had also let him know that even his mistakes weren't going to cause me to step outside of his leadership. The experience of handling an uncomfortable incident with grace and self-control gave me an incredible sense of empowerment and confidence.

I would need that confidence a few weeks later, when a package arrived for my husband while he was out of town. It was a start-up kit for a business he knew I would not have approved of; and he had not only signed up, he had done so without telling me. A double dose of adrenaline shot through my body, as I paced the floor. My thoughts were racing, my lips were pursed, and my heart was pounding. I wanted to call him right then to give him a piece of my mind.

Remembering the incident at the church, I began to wonder if I could handle this situation, too, with Active Submission. Could I prick my husband's conscience, without *being* his conscience? Could I say my peace in a God-pleasing way and let Him handle the rest? There were plenty of things I wanted to say—but most had criticism or chastisement attached to them. Nervously, I dialed the phone.

> *Do not be quick with your mouth, do not be hasty in your heart to utter anything before God. God is in heaven and you are on earth, so let your words be few (Ecclesiastes 5:2).*

After our greetings, I stuck with the facts: "You received a package of products in the mail and a contract for a business arrangement. I don't feel comfortable about this."

"I know," he said, explaining the reasons for his decision. He sounded both defensive and guilty.

When he stopped talking, there was silence. My mind raced, trying to think of what to say next that wouldn't be critical. I wanted to take charge and tell him to cancel the contract; but God wanted me to be his helper, not his leader.

Thinking I was buying time, but in retrospect being led by the Holy Spirit, I asked, "Did you pray about it?"

"No," he replied quietly.

"Would you?" I asked, as a Moment of Leadership.

"Yes," he said.

"If you still believe it is a wise decision after praying, I will honor your decision as the leader of our family." It was a conscious decision to let him lead, but it wasn't as easy as it sounds—wasting money is not something I tolerate well, at least not when it's someone else doing the wasting.

In the end, he did cancel the agreement, but it was his decision. I hadn't forced my will on him. Active Submission had again given me the skills to turn an emotional situation where God wouldn't have been welcomed *("I've got this one, God")* into one where hearts were prepared and He was invited in.

> *Trust in the LORD with all your heart and lean not on your own understanding; in all your ways acknowledge him, and he will make your paths straight (Proverbs 3:5-6).*

CB BO

Here's one final example: a month after the previous incident, my husband and I had to cancel some vacation plans by a certain date, in order to get our deposit back. Since he had made the original reservation, I treated it as a Moment of Leadership by inviting him to take care of the cancellation. That may not have been the smartest thing to do. Moments of Leadership are supposed to be "low-risk, low-emotion" situations where any response is acceptable. In this case, I cared very much what happened, and I had set myself up for disappointment.

Anxiously, I waited as the date came and went. Neither of us said a word. Two days later, I found out he hadn't cancelled. *"How could he have been so stupid?"* I thought. It was as if he had deliberately procrastinated.

Worse, he offered no explanation or apology. If we were going to discuss it, I was going to have to be the one to bring it up, and that made me furious. I tossed and turned all that night.

In your anger do not sin; when you are on your beds, search your hearts and be silent (Psalm 4:4).

I'm not really an angry person, but at that moment, part of me wanted to destroy with my words, tear down what he had done, and grind it into the dust—without regard for our relationship. The other part wanted to handle it in a God-pleasing way, being neither controlling and dominant, nor weak and subservient. When morning came, my husband went into the bathroom to shave. I struggled to hold my tongue, praying:

"Oh Lord direct my footsteps according to your word; let no sin rule over me." I can't be silent. Give me words to say that aren't domineering and hateful, but effective for addressing the situation without destroying our relationship. "May the words of my mouth and the meditation of my heart be pleasing in your sight, O LORD, my Rock and my Redeemer" (Psalm 119:133; 19:14).

Rising up on one elbow, I called out, "You know, we lost that deposit by just a few days." I was trying to state just the facts as calmly as possible, even though I was still struggling with my emotions.

"I know," he said, grudgingly from around the corner—*but that was all he said!* There wasn't a hint of guilt or sorrow.

"Great," I thought. *"Now what?"* I wanted him to acknowledge what he had done and show some remorse. How could I tell him that, without criticizing?

Unable to think of anything, I said, "When I sin against us as a family, I ask for your forgiveness." It was a fact, it was the truth, and there was nothing more to say. I waited. If I wanted my husband to hear God's voice, mine had to be quiet.

After a long pause, he came through the doorway and sat on the edge of the bed. "Will you forgive me?" he asked.

I can't explain why that made everything okay, but it did. It was as if the sun had burst through the clouds and wiped away all bitterness. I was suddenly in love with my husband, again—even more than before—and in awe of God's power. He had accomplished in the stillness what no amount of my noisy chastisement could have done, and a situation that had been capable of ripping a permanent tear in the fabric of our marriage had been stripped of its power, in an instant.

Guilt became repentance, resentment became forgiveness, and destruction became restoration. Our marriage wasn't just spared a trauma—it was enriched, as God revealed Himself to us in a way we hadn't known before. My faith soared. The money I had been so concerned about losing seemed like a very small sacrifice to pay for such an extraordinary gift.

CR BOCR BO

Chapter 16- Suggested Prayers

Prayer for You

Father,

When my husband sins, remind me of my holy calling to be his helper, not his conscience. Keep me focused on You so my mind doesn't wander into self-serving anger and resentment. If it does, convict me quickly, so that I may return to You quickly.

Give me wisdom to see each situation through Your eyes. Put godly words into my mouth and let those words be a catalyst that opens my husband's ears to hear Your voice. Prepare my heart with the willingness to forgive him as you have forgiven me.

May Your living water run continuously through my spirit, that I might be like a *tree that sends out its roots by the stream and does not fear when heat comes (from Jeremiah 17:7-8)*. Make my intentions pure and true, my motivation only to honor and please You by being a light of Your love in my marriage and in the world. In Jesus' name. Amen.

Prayer to Give to Your Husband

Father,

Thank you for giving me my wife—a woman who has chosen to love You and respect me—as my helpmate. Give her wisdom and discernment, compassion and patience, in equal measure. Help her remember that I, too, am a work in progress. In Jesus' name. Amen.

Chapter 16 - Homework

1. In what ways do you think you help your husband?

2. In what ways does your husband say you help him?

3. What, if anything, do you expect from your husband in return? How can you keep those expectations from becoming idols of your heart? Explain why that's difficult.

4. Give an example of how you tried to be your husband's Holy Spirit, or his conscience, this week. Then think of something you could have said instead, that would have been helping, not leading. Role play both with a member of your small group.

5. Memorize Psalm 119:133. Write an example of how you relied on it and used it this week.

17. As Unto the Lord

oward the end of my first year practicing Active Submission, my husband and I seemed to stop growing. We had been making so much progress that it felt like we hit a brick wall: we weren't going backwards, but we weren't going forward, either, and I was frustrated. We had come too far not to experience *everything* God had for marriage. Something more was needed, but what?

"Submit to your husband as unto the Lord."

"I'm already doing that."

"Submit to your husband as unto the Lord."

"I *am* submitting."

"As unto the Lord."

I was confused. God seemed to be telling me the way I submitted to my husband was different than the way I submitted to the Lord. I hadn't thought about it before, but *of course* it was different. I submitted to the Lord because I trusted Him completely. He was perfect; and I had no doubts about His provision, protection, faithfulness, and love. My confidence in Him was so strong that I *delighted* in submitting to Him.

I loved my husband and trusted him, too, but not in *that* way. I submitted to him in order to help him be a godly leader—but only because I trusted in the Lord. If *"submit as unto the Lord"* meant God expected me to trust my husband in the same way I trusted Him, I was in trouble. I had seen too many hearts shipwrecked on those rocky shores. A feeling of dread crept over me: God wanted more than I wanted to give.

Active Submission had been a joy, never a burden; about giving Moments of Leadership, not a life of submission; about the sincerity of my heart, not the sacrifice of my identity. Every step of the way, I had been able to see ahead to the benefits of my obedience. It had been safe—at least compared to this new thing God was asking of me. He wasn't showing me the way ahead, either. He was just pointing to a place that seemed dark, frightening, and forbidding—and saying, "Go."

"But Lord, my husband has given me no evidence he's worthy of such trust."

"Faith is being sure of what we hope for and certain of what we do not see" (Hebrews 11:1).

"So the past year has just been a dress rehearsal for the real thing? Is *that* what You're saying? This is too hard, Lord. *Increase my faith!"* (Luke 17:5).

"If you have faith as small as a mustard seed, you can say to this mulberry tree, 'Be uprooted and planted in the sea,' and it will obey you" (Luke 17:6).

I wanted to please God, but I was scared—and ashamed. If I trusted Him as much as I claimed that I did, why was I hesitating?

> *"Commit your way to the LORD; trust in him and he will do this: He will make your righteousness shine like the dawn, the justice of your cause like the noonday sun" (Psalm 37:5-6).*

"And He will do this . . ." It was a promise that if I committed my way to Him, He would respond faithfully. Was I willing to sacrifice myself on faith alone? Or would I say, *"It's dark, no one sees me" (Isaiah 47:10),* ignore His voice, and go my own way?

> *"I urge you, in view of God's mercy, to offer your bodies as living sacrifices, holy and pleasing to God— this is your spiritual act of worship" (Romans 12:1).*

Months of focusing on pleasing God had brought me into His presence again and again, and I craved more of Him—not less. The thought of not being able to draw near was unbearable. So, with fear and uncertainty pounding in my heart, I nailed my desires and fears to His cross, committing to trust my husband *"as unto the Lord."*

> *"Whoever wants to save his life will lose it, but whoever loses his life for me will find it" (Matthew 16:25).*

Knowing that by the light of day my commitment might seem like a dream and be conveniently "forgotten," I slipped out of bed, composed a note at my desk, and put it in a frame on my husband's bedside table:

> *Your prayers uphold me, your love surrounds me, and your gentle spirit is my strength. As a husband, you are a blessing from God. Yet I have fallen short of being a godly wife. I ask your forgiveness and I commit to you that from today onward, I will submit to you as unto the Lord. I will trust you to provide and care for us, as I trust God and believe that He will provide for us through you.*
>
> *I will stumble and at times slip back into my old fears, but I pray the Holy Spirit will convict me to repentance and trust you will forgive me and help me return to godly living, for there is no joy outside of His commandments.*

I lay back down, but it was impossible to sleep. Emotionally, I felt like I was in a dark swamp, danger and evil reaching out for me from every side. Rehearsing the words I had written, over and over in my head, I kept glancing at the dark silhouette of the frame across the room. It was a radical commitment—maybe too radical. I considered taking it down, but didn't.

Morning came slowly and gently. My husband woke up, read the note, said "That's nice," and went to shave. I don't know what I had expected, but I was relieved and in a strange way, a little disappointed.

Things didn't change overnight. They did change, though. We started experiencing a closeness we had never known before—and our love grew deeper every day. Faith began to define our marriage, and even times of struggle became blessings through which God revealed Himself to us and brought us closer to together. The changes weren't always explainable by earthly laws, but they were always explained spiritually in God's Word.

When my husband and I first met, for example, he looked at me in a way that made me feel beautiful, cherished, and loved. That look had faded with familiarity until, after a few years of marriage, he hardly seemed to notice me at all. I had reassured myself that if he didn't notice the good things, he probably didn't notice the bad things, either, but I missed feeling beautiful in his eyes.

I had tried changing my hair, losing weight, lighting candles—whatever the latest book or magazine said would attract his attention, but nothing had worked. I knew the Bible said we shouldn't be concerned with outer beauty, but that didn't seem like very practical advice in today's world.

> *Your beauty should not come from outward adornment, such as braided hair and the wearing of gold jewelry and fine clothes. Instead, it should be that of your inner self, the unfading beauty of a gentle and quiet spirit, which is of great worth in God's sight. For this is the way the holy women of the past who put their hope in God used to make themselves beautiful. They were submissive to their own husband (1 Peter 3:3-6).*

Those verses reminded of the line, *"Well, at least she's got a great personality."* As nice as it was to think about being beautiful to God, I wanted to be beautiful to my husband, too—and society and the media determined that, not scripture. That was what I thought, anyway.

Then, one day, *that look* came back. It had matured and softened some—the excitement of the unknown was replaced by the glow of pride—but it was there, nonetheless. He began to linger when he passed by. He stopped to caress my hair or give me a kind word. He smiled when he kissed me good-bye. He looked me in the eyes when we talked!

At first I thought he was just trying to be more Christ-like by *overlooking* my physical shortcomings; but it soon became clear he was actually seeing me *differently*. Yet, the only thing different about me was my commitment to submit to him *as unto the Lord*. Nothing on the outside had changed.

Or maybe it had. Other people started telling me I looked different—beautiful, even. I read the scripture in Peter again, and that's when I realized I hadn't read it closely enough, before. It said, "For this is the way the holy women of the past *made themselves beautiful*." Peter didn't say they just *looked* beautiful. He said they *were* beautiful.

Something had happened, something beyond explanation in the earthly sense, and so contrary to my understanding of the world, I wouldn't have believed it if I hadn't experienced it. The joy of the Lord and the beauty of Christ had overcome the imperfections of my body, skin, and bone, to make me beautiful in my husband's eyes. It was God's beauty secret, revealed in His Word all along, but overlooked because His thoughts and ways were so much higher than my own.

17. As Unto the Lord

> *"My thoughts are not your thoughts, neither are your ways my ways," declares the LORD (Isaiah 55:8).*

CB ED

Women often say to me, "If my husband would do what the Bible says and love me as an equal heir, then I could submit to him." However, the submission commands *always* come before the love commands, every time (look in the Appendix). I believe it's not a coincidence, but God's way of telling us that a man is *unable* to love his wife the way God intends, *unless* she is submitting to him in an active, godly way. A husband's disobedience is not an excuse for a wife's disobedience . . . it's all the more reason why she should strive to please God.

That's proven true in my marriage, as well as in the marriages of other women who have practiced Active Submission. Whenever we created opportunities for our husbands to lead, they became more loving. Sometimes the change was dramatic, sometimes it was subtle, but it was always there with enough evidence to inspire us to greater confidence and faith in God's Word.

On the other hand, when we slipped back into our old dominating habits, our husbands reverted to their grumpy, angry, or withdrawn ways with remarkable speed. As one woman said, "I realize, now, how I choose to act determines how my husband responds and how my marriage goes."

She didn't mean she could control her husband. She meant she was so confident of God's faithfulness she wasn't afraid to obey His commands—knowing that, through her obedience, God would work in her husband and bless their marriage.

> *O LORD Almighty, blessed is the woman who*
> *trusts in you (from Psalm 84:12).*

Lately, I've begun to understand how absurd it was for me to ever doubt that God could bless me through my husband. Was my husband stronger than God? Could he prevent God from carrying out His intentions for me?

When I chose to trust my husband *as unto the Lord* and asked God to bless me through him, it was as if to say, *"God, You're going to have to go through him to get to me."* Like red water being poured through white sand, or the blood of Christ through the heart of a man, there was no way God's power would move through my husband to me without changing him—and *us*.

The Bible says that when a man and woman unite, they become one flesh. I believe that one flesh, like every individual, has a God-shaped hole in it which, when not filled, creates a sense of emptiness or longing. I used to call it a spiritual "limp" that weighed down our marriage, because it was so distinct and yet so impossible to satisfy in our own strength.

As I grew in my understanding of godly submission, the hole in our marriage was filled by God, an experience every bit as life-changing as when our individual God-shaped holes were filled. The emptiness left, the longing was satisfied, and our marriage became a new creation in Christ, empowered by the Holy Spirit and transformed by the love of God.

*You see that your faith and your actions were
working together, and your faith was made complete
by what you did (from James 2:22).*

CB ⅋Ɔ

Marriage was created by God as a foreshadowing and
constant reminder of the Gospel: a pictorial representation of
the call to leave our dependency on the world (mother and
father) and become one with Christ. It also represents Christ's
authority over the Church.

*For the husband is the head of the wife as Christ is
the head of the church . . . For this reason a man will
leave his father and mother and be united to his wife,
and the two will become one flesh. This is a profound
mystery—but I am talking about Christ and the church
(Ephesians 5:23, 31-32, quoting Genesis 2:24).*

It's not hard to find evidence of the disastrous
consequences when the Church isn't obeying God's command
to submit to Christ. The same is true when a wife isn't obeying
the command to give her husband headship of the family. Then,
the marriage no longer reflects the Gospel or the Church.
Stripped of its spiritual significance and purpose, it becomes an
empty shell, good for nothing but to be thrown out and trampled
by men—which is exactly what we're being faced with today.

*If the salt loses its saltiness, how can it be made
salty again? It is no longer good for anything, except
to be thrown out and trampled by men (Matt. 5:13).*

Current generations unknowingly speak the truth when they reject marriage as "just a piece of paper." God Himself might say the same thing about what *we* call marriage, when He considers what we have done with it. That may sound harsh, but it's true. The worst attack is not coming from those who dismiss marriage or try to change its definition. The worst attack is coming from within—from our failure to trust in God and obey Him in the way we consider our *own* marriages.

C33 80

It was not by accident you were born into this generation of spiritual warfare against marriage and faith. It was not by chance you married the man you are now married to. And it was not by coincidence you picked up this book. God has been preparing you every step of the way for the calling He has on your life.

> *Whoever can be trusted with very little can also be trusted with much (Luke 16:10a).*

There is no greater joy than doing what God wants you to do. And what does He want for you? The answer is in the Bible. So believe, trust, and obey. Let Him transform your marriage into the glorious Christ-reflecting experience He meant for it to be, then go and teach others to do the same. You are a daughter of the King: *"Who knows but that you have come to royal position for such a time as this?"* (Esther 4:14).

Make your life count, now—*as unto the Lord.*

C3 80C3 80

Prologue

or years, I prayed so hard I thought my heart would break, "Dear God, *please* change my husband." I couldn't understand why He wasn't answering that prayer. It wasn't until I took "changing my husband" off the throne of my heart and put "pleasing God" on it that things started happening. Only when I redirected my worship and prayers in that way and started asking Him to change me, did things begin to happen.

God designed my husband to be the head of our family, but he couldn't step into that leadership position until I was willing to give it to him. God has blessed my husband through the changes He made in me—and He has blessed me in the most amazing and surprising ways through the changes he has made in my husband. We're both works in progress. Neither of us is perfect, but there's such pleasure in the journey now, our entire perspective on marriage, life, and faith has changed. If you told me now that I could have either a perfectly godly husband right away, or one to share the journey of becoming more like Christ with, I would take the latter.

Life is characterized today, not by our accomplishments or our activities, but by the joy of learning to obey God together and experience His blessings through trusting in Him. Naturally, we stumble, but as we've drawn closer to the Lord the power of Christ's love has poured through our hearts, growing our love for each other deeper and richer than either of us could have ever imagined.

It is that very thing which I hope and pray for you. It's so tempting to read a book, try a few things, have a few successes, and then return to old habits. I desire more for you than that. My prayer is that God's Word will so demonstrate His power in your marriage and become part of who you are, that you will be forever changed—and never go back. Active Submission is not a solution to a problem marriage, it's a life change.

Let me know how I can help you in your teaching, and send me your testimonies of praise as you practice Active Submission and Moments of Leadership. God bless you and keep you in His Spirit, now and forevermore.

> *Do not merely listen to the word, and so deceive yourselves. Do what it says.*
>
> *Anyone who listens to the word but does not do what it says is like a woman who looks at her face in a mirror and, after looking at herself, goes away and immediately forgets what she looks like.*
>
> *But the woman who looks intently into the perfect law that gives freedom, and continues to do this, not forgetting what she has heard, but doing it—she will be blessed in what she does (from James 1:22-25).*

Karen Haught
kbhaught@godempowered.com

Believe. Trust. Obey.

If you love Me, you will obey what I command (John 14:15).

Appendix - Scripture References

Ephesians 5:22-30

"Wives, submit to your husbands as unto the Lord. For the husband is the head of the wife as Christ is the head of the church, his body, of which he is the Savior. Now as the church submits to Christ, so also wives should submit to their husbands in everything.

"Husbands, love your wives, just as Christ loved the church and gave himself up for her to make her holy, cleansing her by the washing with water through the word, and to present her to himself as a radiant church, without stain or wrinkle or any other blemish, but holy and blameless.

"In this same way, husbands ought to love their wives as their own bodies. He who loves his wife loves himself. After all, no one ever hated his own body, but he feeds and cares for it, just as Christ does the church— for we are members of his body."

Colossians 3:18-19

"Wives, submit to your husbands, as is fitting in the Lord."
"Husbands, love your wives and do not be harsh with them."

1 Peter 3:1-9

"Wives, in the same way be submissive to your husbands so that, if any of them do not believe the word, they may be won over without words by the behavior of their wives, when they see the purity and reverence of your lives.

"Your beauty should not come from outward adornment, such as braided hair and the wearing of gold jewelry and fine clothes. Instead, it should be that of your inner self, the unfading beauty of a gentle and quiet spirit, which is of great worth in God's sight.

"For this is the way the holy women of the past who put their hope in God used to make themselves beautiful. They were submissive to their own husbands, like Sarah, who obeyed Abraham and called him her master. You are her daughters if you do what is right and do not give way to fear.

"Husbands, in the same way be considerate as you live with your wives, and treat them with respect as the weaker partner and as heirs with you of the gracious gift of life, so that nothing will hinder your prayers."

 C8 80C8 80

Biography

Karen Haught spent thirty years in the corporate world, first as an entrepreneur and then as an executive in both public and private companies, before becoming a certified biblical counselor in 2007. Her first book, "The God Empowered® Wife: How Strong Women Can Help Their Husbands Become Godly Leaders," (2008) has helped transform marriages around the world.

As a speaker, Karen is well-known for incorporating lively demonstrations, true stories, and case studies into her workshops and conferences—which she has shared with audiences across the USA as well as Asia-Pacific, Europe, Australia, and Africa. Karen and her husband live in Houston, Texas, where they are both active in their local church.

This book came out of her experiences, beginning in 2005, as she learned to apply the principles of biblical counseling to her marriage and help others do the same.

National and international speaking engagements:
kbhaught@godempowered.com

Thank You

My husband, Jim, for his wisdom, faithfulness, love, prayers, provision, and friendship.

Jay Adams, Randy Patten, and the National Association of Nouthetic Counselors (www.nanc.org).

Faith Biblical Counseling Ministries in Lafayette, Indiana.

Graphic artist, Jerry Cooley, for cover design and title.

Photographer and writer, Kristi Sberna, for back cover photo.

Scripture Index

Endnotes

[1] Thomas, Gary, Sacred Marriage. Zondervan, Grand Rapids, MI. 2000.

[2] The initial paragraphs of the historical survey were adapted from Robert Lewis' Men's Fraternity program, The Quest for Authentic Manhood. Lifeway Press. Nashville, TN. 2006.

[3] "The Greatest Generation" was first coined in Tom Brokaw's book by the same name. Published by The Random House, 1998.

[4] Reddy, Helen and Burton, Ray. "I am Woman." Capitol Records, 1972.

[5] Spock, Benjamin. Baby and Child Care. Available in many different editions from a variety of publishers.

[6] "The American Dream" was first coined by James Truslow Adams in 1931.http://en.wikipedia.org/wiki/American_Dream.

[7] My son's father died unexpectedly of a heart attack when I was in my fifth marriage and our son was twenty-one. He found him on the floor beside his bed.

[8] More on our nature as worshippers: Instruments in the Redeemer's Hands, by Paul David Tripp. P & R Publishing, 2002.

[9] The "Liar, Thief, Blasphemer" evangelism section is from Hell's Best Kept Secret, by Ray Comfort. Whitaker House. 2004. Used by permission. www.livingwaters.com.

[10] This section, forward, is the author's.

[11] "The Family Prayer Song." ©1994 Marantha Praise, Inc./ASCAP (Administered by Music Services). All rights reserved. Used with permission.

[12] Grace Murray Hopper, programmer and inventor of COBOL is said to have coined this phrase (www.thinkexist.com).

[13] Omartian, Stormie. The Power of a Praying Wife. Harvest House Publishers. Eugene, OR. 1997.

[14] Mack, Wayne. Anger & Stress Management, God's Way. Calvary Press. 2004.

[15] More on sin as the root of the human condition: Seeing with New Eyes, by David Powlison. P & R Publishing, 2003. Also How People Change, by David Lane and Paul Tripp. New Growth Press, 2006.

[16] Sande, Ken. The Peacemaker: A Biblical Guide to Resolving Personal Conflict, by Ken Sande. Baker Books. Grand Rapids, MI. 2005. pp. 115-116

[17] Adams, Jay. A Theology of Christian Counseling. Zondervan. Grand Rapids, MI., 2005, p 145.

Notes:

Made in the USA
Middletown, DE
28 November 2018